THE SECRET WAR

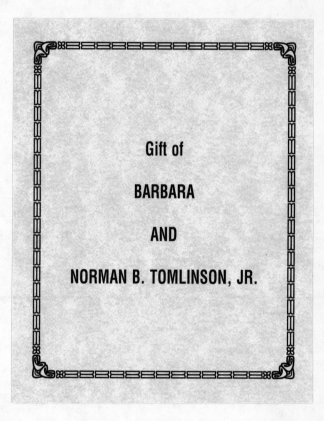

THE
SECRET WAR

CIA covert operations against Cuba 1959-62

By Fabián Escalante

Translated by Maxine Shaw

Edited by Mirta Muñiz

OCEAN PRESS

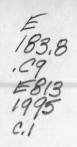
Cover design by David Spratt

ISBN 1-875284-86-9

First printed 1995

Printed in Australia

Published by Ocean Press,
GPO Box 3279, Melbourne, Victoria 3001, Australia

Distributed in the United States by the Talman Company,
131 Spring Street, New York, NY 10012, USA
Distributed in Britain and Europe by Central Books,
99 Wallis Road, London E9 5LN, Britain
Distributed in Australia by Astam Books,
57-61 John Street, Leichhardt, NSW 2040, Australia
Distributed in Cuba and Latin America by Ocean Press,
Apartado 686, C.P. 11300, Havana, Cuba
Distributed in Southern Africa by
Phambili Agencies, 52 Jeppe Street, Johannesburg 2001, South Africa

✠ *Contents* ✠

To Teresita, my indefatigable companion who has helped me so much in this undertaking;

to my children Raúl and César, who assisted with their opinions;

to Etcheverry, Roque and Ramón, whose collaboration was invaluable;

to Mirta, David, Deborah and Luisito, whose advice, suggestions and personal effort as the editors and publishers was crucial;

and finally, to my comrades in struggle, the true heroes of this epic.

About the author

Division General Fabián Escalante Font was born in the city of Havana, Cuba, in 1940. At a very young age he suffered persecution and was imprisoned for his activities against the dictatorship of Fulgencio Batista. With the triumph of the revolutionary movement in 1959, he joined the newly-created State Security forces, where he carried out varied activities against counterrevolutionary organizations and the Central Intelligence Agency of the United States, including the latter's Operation AM/LASH.

He directed the investigations which the Cuban government carried out at the request of the U.S. House of Representatives Select Committee when the investigation into the assassination of President John F. Kennedy was reopened in 1978.

Between 1976 and 1982 he was chief of the State Security Department (G-2). He headed the Political Office of the Interior Ministry from 1985 to 1989; was a member of the Central Committee from 1980 to 1991; and a deputy in the National Assembly until 1992. He is presently an adviser to the Minister of the Interior.

In 1991 and 1992 he formed part of the Cuban delegation that attended the tripartite meetings (Soviet Union-USA-Cuba) in Antigua and Havana to discuss and analyze the antecedents, causes and consequences of the Missile Crisis of October 1962.

In 1992 he published *Girón, la gran conjura* [The Bay of Pigs, the great conspiracy], where he analyzed the subversive events that led up to the mercenary invasion in April 1961.

In 1993 he published his second book, *Cuba: La guerra secreta de la CIA* [Cuba, the secret war of the CIA], which narrates the main subversive activities of the United States against Cuba in the period from 1959 to 1962. This is a translation of his revised version of that book.

He has contributed to other national publications and has given lectures on these topics.

Preface

There are two aspects to the United States' war of aggression against Cuba, a war which has persisted for more than a third of a century and often without clearly defined limits. Firstly, there is the clandestine offensive, described in great detail by one of the major players in the conflict, Division General Fabián Escalante, chief of a Cuban counterintelligence unit in the period recounted in this book, and later head of the Cuban State Security Department. This is the history of the United States' clandestine actions against the triumphant revolution on the neighboring island with the aim of resubmitting it to the political, military and economic domination to which it had been subject since the Spanish colonial power was overthrown at the end of the 19th century. It is the dark chapter dealing with subversive operations and conspiracies to launch military attacks by air, land and sea; of infiltration by CIA agents for the purpose of committing sabotage and attempting to assassinate the most well-known leaders of the revolution, above all, Fidel Castro. It is the story of the complicity and submission of other Latin American governments and the vassalage of discontented elements in Cuba in the service of the imperialist plans against their own country.

The other aspect of this all-out war is the diplomatic intrigue; the economic blockade which seeks to starve the people of the island into surrender; the propaganda and disinformation campaigns waged by the media under the direct or indirect control of the United States; and the use of international organizations to isolate the Cuban revolution in hope of leaving it defenseless and weakened as a prelude to a final bellicose act.

In essence, these two methods of war overlap, although their connection is not always publicly clear. As this book recalls, when the U.S. Senate established the Central Intelligence Agency in 1947, the National Security Council issued a directive giving the Agency the authority to carry out covert actions, defined as "activity which is meant to further the sponsoring nation's foreign policy objectives, and to be concealed in order to permit that nation to plausibly deny responsibility."[1] In the case of Cuba, however, due to the hysteria which has always accompanied the U.S. policy, rarely — if ever — has any of this aggression been able to be presented as acceptable policy in the light of international law, treaty commitments signed by the United States, the principles and stipulations of the Charter of the United Nations or the regional Organization of American States. The various U.S. administrations have never been able to deny their responsibility in the implementation of this policy against Cuba. Moreover, not only have they been unable to deny it, but their intentions have always been quickly unmasked, leaving no valid justification for their illegal acts, in clear opposition to international public opinion.

From the inception of this policy of aggression, both the executive orders of the White House and the laws passed through the Congress have had their counterparts in the CIA plans and vice versa. It is not clear whether these laws and presidential orders were based on the subversive plans of the CIA or whether the CIA's plans were in response to the presidential orders and Congressional bills. There is no doubt, however, that the CIA has served as the launch pad of a huge plan conceived for the purpose of destroying the Cuban revolution, and this book provides the facts to prove this point. It shows how in the course of more than three decades, the original policy has not deviated from its course.

---

[1] *Alleged assassination plots involving foreign leaders.* Senate Report No. 94-465. 94th Congress. 1st Session, November 18, 1975 (Washington D.C.: U.S. Government Printing Office, 1975), 9.

The only variation, in deference to the different permutations of U.S. domestic policy, has been the rhetoric used against Cuba, sometimes strident and vicious and other times low-key and moderate, while the CIA has been ever-present in one form or another at the head or behind the attacks suffered by Cuba.

These pages tell the real story of the CIA operations against Cuba in the first years after the triumph of the revolution in 1959, when the United States turned all its force against the island. The facts herein are based on documents taken from the Cuban State Security files and others declassified by the Central Intelligence Agency itself. But these dramatic deeds do not read like a dry legal record, since the text transcends the clamor of the struggle between the great aggressive power and the nation which is its intended victim. The confessions of the leaders of these U.S.-backed operations come alive on these pages, especially when one remembers that, after all, the war is not yet over. The book also sheds light on the intelligence duel between the two contenders, in one case to put into practice its aggressive and destabilizing policy; and in the other the enormous efforts to protect itself from the traps and trickery of the adversary.

The story told in this book has the virtue of presenting the concrete facts without glossing them over or touching them up or presenting them second hand. The author narrates the events exactly as they occurred, with all the force which springs from the very sources of the protagonists in the dispute. The agents who infiltrated the coasts of Cuba in order to organize an insurrection parade through this text, along with the penetrations of Cuban security agents into the enemy groups organized one after the other by the CIA, frustrating subversive plan after subversive plan. A clear picture emerges of the infighting among the various sectors of the CIA which supported the different counterrevolutionary groups, each with their own aspirations for power with the triumph of their military plans; the hiding of some projects from the U.S. President himself, as happened before the Playa Girón (Bay of Pigs) invasion, for example; the airlifts of arms, explosives and equipment into Cuban territory by U.S. aircraft; the role of the Pentagon in the plans for a military attack; and the involvement of the Mafia in attempted assassinations in the hope of recovering the lucrative profits they obtained in Cuba before the revolution in gambling casinos, drugs and prostitution. Almost like a black comedy, the Cuban authorities again and again upset the plans of the CIA. On countless occasions Cuban security agents participated in the most intimate clandestine meetings of the subversive groups, thus uncovering their plots.

The author does not attempt to chronicle the entire secret war of the CIA against Cuba, among other reasons because much evidence of these activities is still buried in the files and because, as is obvious, the conflict is still not over. Nevertheless, this book provides an indispensable contribution to understanding the extent of the diabolical mechanisms put into play for the purpose of reversing history and the risks of this unfinished but nevertheless frustrated battle against the revolutionary forces and people of Cuba who zealously and fervently struggle to preserve intact the independence of their country.

Carlos Lechuga

CHAPTER 1

An ugly American

The silver color of the plane was brightly reflected in the light of the September sun on the runway at Havana's Rancho Boyeros Airport. The four-motor Pan American airliner pulled into its parking spot, the stairway was affixed, and an assortment of passengers in a variety of clothing began to descend — some were smiling, some frowning, some indifferent, some self-absorbed. Among them was the sleek figure of a blond stewardess, the strong Havana sun forcing her to nearly close her eyes while they adjusted to the sudden blast of tropical light. From atop the staircase, she signaled to two uniformed stewards waiting on the ground, who hurried up the steps, understanding their instructions. Minutes later they came back down, carrying in their arms a tall, broad-shouldered man, who also squinted in the sun. Rushing behind them came someone with a wheelchair, to which the man was long resigned since his bout with polio, although this experience could not but influence his opinions and decisions in his important job as Inspector General of the CIA.

An elderly woman regarded him with pity, and in the distance a dog barked at a tanker truck which had started up its motor to go out and refuel the plane which just arrived.

The year was 1958 and the man was Lyman Kirkpatrick, whose mission was to assist the dictator Fulgencio Batista to evaluate the the political and military state of the country. He also proposed interviewing businessmen, and social and public figures, in short, representatives of the key sectors of the society, to get a first-hand assessment of the stability of the regime his country protected. Finally, he wanted to review the work of the dictatorship's various police bodies, in particular an apparatus created a short while earlier in the heat of the Cold War: the Bureau for the Repression of Communist Activities (BRAC), whose task was to eliminate revolutionary ideas, with the support of the CIA and the FBI.

He was assisted by a veteran spy at the U.S. embassy, a diplomatic attaché named William Caldwell, who had spent his entire CIA career in Latin America, cultivating relations with local police. Kirkpatrick knew from his own experience that these organizations were, in the end, the bulwark which propped up the regimes which reigned on the continent, the backbone of U.S. investment.

The United States had important interests in Cuba. As John F. Kennedy commented, "At the beginning of 1959, U.S. companies owned about 40 percent of the Cuban sugar lands, almost all the cattle ranches, 90 percent of the mines and mineral concessions, 80 percent of the utilities and practically all the oil industry, and supplied two-thirds of Cuba's imports."[2] The volume of its investments in those years amounted to a billion dollars, a very high figure indeed considering that its total investment in Latin America at the time was only around $8 billion. Political events in the country presaged a social upheaval with inevitable repercussions for U.S. interests, and this was the main reason Kirkpatrick had come to Havana to better inform himself about the storm clouds gathering over Cuba.

Kirkpatrick was first taken to the dictator's mansion, located in the old part of the city, where he had to rely on the services of soldiers to help him up the staircase of that imposing building. He almost fell several times, and swearing, he finally arrived upstairs where an aide-de-camp of the dictator waited to take him to a meeting. The soldier rolled the wheelchair rapidly into the President's office. Inside were Batista, General Francisco

---

[2] *The speeches of Senator John F. Kennedy's presidential campaign of 1960* (Washington D.C.: U.S. Government Printing Office, 1961), 513.

Tabernilla, chief of the Army, and Colonel Mariano Faget, commander of the BRAC.

Batista was the consummate artist. He assumed the right posture for every occasion and, with a theatrical gesture, after an exchange of cordialities and an interminable bout of handshaking, he turned the meeting over to Tabernilla, who spread a large map on the table and began explaining: "This is the Sierra Maestra. Fidel Castro and his communists are in the most dense and mountainous zones and, as you can see, they are surrounded. We are going to bomb them until they come out of their dens and we can assure you that the days of these scoundrels are numbered."

Batista smiled benevolently at his man, displaying an air of absolute tranquillity. Tabernilla, taking advantage of this atmosphere, continued saying, "I understand the concerns which exist in the United States over the prolonging of our military campaign against the rebels, but this is because we didn't take them seriously at first. When they first landed we practically annihilated them, and we assumed that was the end of it. . ."

He continued in this vein for more than an hour. Batista directed various meaningful glances at the general until the latter closed his lips with an obsequious smile. Then he turned to Faget, a man of neat and tidy appearance who explained in detail the operations of his group of "experts." They were only concerned with the communists, he said. They applied the methods they had been taught in U.S. training schools, and if on occasion excesses were committed, it was due to the zeal of their subordinates. Anything heard to the contrary was just talk and political propaganda to smear the image of the government.

If you were to believe these men the situation was under control and Fidel Castro's guerrillas in the mountains and the dissidents in the cities would soon be wiped out. Kirkpatrick asked a number of questions. He wanted details about the number of rebels who operated in the Sierra Maestra, the communist forces in the cities, the control of the workers' movement, the situation in the schools and universities — in short, he poked around in all the corners where a force that could precipitate the fall of Batista's military government might be lurking.[3]

That evening he met with Ambassador Earl Smith[4] and his collaborators. They supported the assessment that the government was going through a rough period but could survive if the United States would open its hand a little and send more weapons and the counterinsurgency advisers it had promised. The local CIA chief reported on his relationship with the police and the "American technicians" under his control. His only concern related to some complaints brought to the attention of the embassy about abuses of power on the part of several police authorities, but he attributed this to the prolonged struggle against the "communists."

However, other prominent Cubans contradicted this view. They predicted the fall of Batista and insisted that the U.S. government should take steps to disassociate itself from the dictator as soon as possible. These opinions were in direct contrast to the calmness presented by the Batista government and the position taken by the U.S. embassy.

Kirkpatrick needed a reliable source of information, someone impartial. So he sent a cable to CIA headquarters in Langley, Virginia, asking to make contact with an agent with a deep cover and with access to political information. The following day he received a response. He was to look up David Atlee Phillips, a

---

[3] Warren Hinckle and William Turner, *Deadly secrets: The CIA-Mafia war against Castro and the assassination of JFK* (New York: Thunder's Mouth Press, 1993), 56-58.

[4] John Dorschner and Roberto Fabricio, *The winds of December* (New York: Coward, McCann & Geoghegan, 1980), 48-51. Also, Michael R. Beschloss, *The crisis years* (New York: Edward Burlingame Books, 1991), 99. John F. Kennedy met with Earl Smith in Havana in December 1957, and although it is not likely that he was familiar with the problems of the dictatorship, he did relate to Cubans. According to George Smathers, he liked the people, which perhaps led him to his conclusion in 1960 that the Batista regime was one of the most bloody and repressive dictatorships in the long history of Latin American repression.

U.S. businessman based in Havana as head of a public relations office and with close ties to the country's media and intelligentsia.

The Agency had learned a lesson from the Guatemalan revolution in the early 1950s when a nationalist government expropriated the land and the public service enterprises of U.S. monopolies to the benefit of the peasants and the population in general. This experience gave rise to a program of infiltrating agents into countries convulsed by "communist ideas" to complement the information received from their embassies.

Phillips was a specialist in Latin American affairs. He was recruited by the CIA in 1950 in Chile where he ran a local newspaper, because of his position, cover and access as a businessman who, along with his wife, had a good command of Spanish. A lifelong patron of the theater with a personable manner, he easily moved into the circles he wished to penetrate. He was a veteran of the Guatemala affair, where he directed the psychological warfare campaign, an integral part of the overthrow of that government.[5]

The meeting took place in a safe house, located in the Berlitz Language School building in the central location of 23rd Street in the populous Vedado neighborhood. At the appointed time, in one of the rooms at the school, Phillips was waiting with his characteristic confident smile.

The interview lasted for more than two hours, and the agent informed his superior in detail of his impressions of the government and the sociopolitical situation of the country. Batista no longer had the forces to control the revolutionaries, Phillips affirmed. He said the economy was in shambles and foreign businessmen no longer wanted to invest in a place where they didn't know what the situation would be from day to day. The United States needed to distance itself from the regime, he asserted, perhaps to support a political force clearly allied with its interests. He suggested Carlos Prío's men Sanchez Arango and

---

[5] David Atlee Phillips, *The night watch* (New York: Ballantine Books), 1, 2, 37. Also Hinckle and Turner, *Deadly secrets*, 56-58.

Tony Varona, who could return representing the legitimacy of the government deposed by the 1952 coup.

The Inspector General looked attentive, leaned his head against the back of his chair, and responded, "I myself have thought of that solution, but the opposition in Washington could be strong. I think that some of the authorities are very committed to Batista, Ambassador Smith for example. . . But the idea of the *Auténticos* is a good one. We can suggest it."

They both agreed, and Kirkpatrick concluded his interview satisfied in having encountered an intelligent official with an interesting perspective. After the meeting he went to the embassy and sent a telegram of the highest priority where he explained his impressions of the visit and his growing doubts about the possibility of Batista continuing in power.

At the Langley headquarters a debate began that would take months to resolve. Colonel J.C. King was chief of the CIA's Western Hemisphere Division and he resolutely opposed any change in U.S. policy toward the regime in Havana. Batista was a "strongman" and this was the only way to govern in Latin America. King's years in Argentina, where he served as military attaché at the embassy, had taught him this. He knew a great many military figures and police who had later become government leaders and established "peace and stability."

However, the officials in the Directorate of Intelligence did not share this point of view.[6] Perhaps that was what led CIA Director Allen Dulles to take a seemingly contradictory position. He thought that authoritarian regimes should be supported, while at the same time encouraging elements in the ranks of the opposition — just in case it should become necessary.

In the case of Cuba, the Agency had taken this precaution, and already had infiltrated several agents among the revolutionaries. There was a top secret force marauding in the Sierra Maestra, led by another American, but in different guise: a "Rambo" in the style of the best Hollywood movie superhero. He was Frank Angelo Fiorini, better known as Frank Sturgis. In

---

[6] Ronald Kessler, *Inside the CIA*, (New York: Pocket Books, 1992), 36.

the 1950s the CIA had linked him up with Carlos Prío in Florida, whose trust he had won. There he established relations with exiles seeking arms and resources in Latin America for the Cuban rebels.

In Mexico he met Pedro Luis Díaz Lanz, a Cuban pilot, who was later a traitor to the Cuban revolution. Díaz Lanz was involved in the revolutionary movement and was in Mexico raising money and arms to send to the rebels in the Sierra Maestra. Sturgis' bluster soon won him the favor of Díaz Lanz, who began to include him in his secret forays to the island. In August 1958 his opportunity finally came. His superiors at the CIA had been pressuring him to make direct contact with Fidel Castro's *barbudos* and evaluate their true political intentions, just in case they happened to overthrow Batista.

A small aircraft was readied in a secret airport in Mexico and Sturgis was enlisted as Díaz Lanz's copilot on a mission to transport an important contraband shipment of arms to Cuba. The day arrived, and on August 28 they landed successfully in a place known as Cayo Espino near the Sierra Maestra. However, Batista's Air Force, which had been tipped off by their agents in Mexico, kept the region under constant surveillance and discovered the plane on the tiny improvised airstrip. They destroyed it with machine gun fire and Díaz Lanz and Sturgis had to temporarily join the guerrilla band operating in that area. They soon found a way out of the country and returned to Mexico, where Sturgis continued his surveillance.

Taking advantage of the circumstances, Robert Wiecha, U.S. consul in Santiago de Cuba and also a CIA official, set up a meeting with Sturgis to learn about his recent experiences with the rebels so as to respond to the insistent demands of the CIA station in Havana. The interview took place in the bar of the centrally located Hotel Casa Granda, where Sturgis was staying.[7] It was an ideal place because, in spite of the repression unleashed by the government, nobody would consider it unusual that two North Americans got together for a couple of drinks. The case

---

[7] Report from Cuban State Security.

officer went directly to the point and asked if Fidel Castro was a communist or a fellow-traveler?

Sturgis leaned back in his seat and responded that Castro was not a communist, although some of those close to him were. He asserted that they could be neutralized in due time since there were very capable men who were faithful friends of the cause and who were being prepared for a future provisional government. He noted that since the United States insisted on supporting Batista, and since the bombs falling every day in the mountains were inscribed "made in USA," a great deal of resentment had been built up. He cited the need to get rid of the regime and support democratic revolutionaries in order to avoid an uncontrollable social explosion fired by anti-American sentiment.

The consul observed the man carefully. He was a professional soldier of fortune. After World War II he had been a policeman in an obscure midwestern town. He couldn't deal with the tranquillity and reenlisted in the service in the intelligence branch. While stationed in Germany he was recruited by the CIA and became a seasoned agent. His assessment of the situation could be trusted.

Wiecha inquired if he recommended supporting Fidel Castro as a possible option for government? Yes, Sturgis replied, conditioning the support on forming a provisional government including prominent figures in business and society who had broken with Batista.

The meeting concluded, and each of them returned to their posts. The general headquarters of the CIA received a coded telegram presenting Sturgis' opinions, and those of the case officer who, taking advantage of the opportunity to make a veiled criticism of his bosses, backed him up.

Toward the end of 1957 a new guerrilla front had been organized in the Escambray mountains, located in the strategic central province of Las Villas, headed by Eloy Gutiérrez Menoyo and a group of his followers. Eloy Gutiérrez had earned political merit in the shadow of his brother Carlos, who was killed in the attack on the Presidential Palace on March 13 of that year when the forces of the Revolutionary Directorate attempted to assassinate Batista. After that action, Gutiérrez Menoyo took advantage of the Directorate's plans to initiate an armed struggle in the Escambray mountains. He took over the plans underway and took up arms with a group of his men, mainly from the ranks of the *Auténticos*, and thus founded the pompously named "Second National Front of the Escambray" for one expressed purpose: to stop the revolutionary movement headed by Fidel Castro which was advancing from the eastern provinces.

Nevertheless, their predatory activities in the Escambray earned them the name of the "beef eaters" and undermined their support. A sign at the entrance to Gutiérrez Menoyo's camp proclaimed his real "patriotic" sentiments: NO COMMUNISTS ALLOWED.

The CIA knew of the planned uprising from the beginning. In reality, the project was in line with their immediate interests. The atmosphere on the island was too charged and this could provide a small escape valve for some of the tensions that could be immediately closed again through some political subterfuge. Moreover, Fidel Castro's rebels in the eastern mountains were strengthening their positions daily, and should Batista's army be swept away by a sea of olive green, Gutiérrez Menoyo's men could serve as a kind of retaining wall.

For these reasons the CIA appointed several agents to occupy leadership positions in Gutiérrez Menoyo's band, among them William Alexander Morgan, a U.S. mercenary whose mission was to rise to second in command of those troops. But Morgan was undisciplined and reported little, greatly displeasing the CIA station, which complained about him constantly. Colonel King subsequently sent another of his agents to act as a contact with the volatile and unstable Morgan. He was an Italian American named John Maples Spiritto, recruited in the early 1950s in Mexico, where the CIA station had used him to infiltrate Fidel Castro's forces when they were preparing the liberation expedition would take them back to Cuban soil at the end of 1956.[8]

---

[8] Report from Cuban State Security files on John Maples Spiritto.

Spiritto was called to CIA headquarters and after a rapid briefing sent to Cuba, where he waited for his contacts to take him to the mountain range in the center of the island.

The encounter between the two Americans in the Escambray was a stormy one. Morgan didn't want to be controlled. He had recruited Eloy Gutiérrez Menoyo and the other chiefs of the organization and he didn't want to share the glory of victory. He was set on becoming an important political figure after they triumphed, and then selling the favors of his government. Finally, Spiritto won him over, threatening to inform the CIA station in Havana of his behavior. Morgan introduced him to Gutiérrez Menoyo and he was given the rank of captain on his very first day in camp. The Second Front situation was sobering, even for someone with as few political scruples as Spiritto. After conversing with most of the officers of that self-appointed "army," he informed the U.S. embassy that they could expect little military success from those forces. The ambitions of the leaders to control a zone of operation provoked daily disputes and their "military" forays amounted to little more than extortion of the local peasants.

Nevertheless, from a political point of view, their stance was anticommunist and they formed part of the barrier that could impede the advance of the troops under Camilo Cienfuegos and Che Guevara toward the western part of the country.

The CIA's appraisal of the Second Front of the Escambray coincided with Spiritto's evaluation. Everything depended on the right propaganda, so that the people of Cuba might learn of these "liberators" and give them their support should the dictatorship be overthrown by insurrection. A public relations agency in the United States was hired for this purpose and David Atlee Phillips received precise instructions for his collaborators to follow in the mass media in Havana.

In the last few days of December 1958, the U.S. embassy was frantic, trying to hold back the revolutionary tide that threatened to sweep away the regime, since Batista's army was already practically defeated. The troops commanded by Fidel Castro and Juan Almeida, together with the forces of the Second Eastern

Front under Commander Raúl Castro in the northern part of Oriente Province, were closing in on the city of Santiago de Cuba. The columns headed by Camilo Cienfuegos and Che Guevara had already reached the Escambray and northern Las Villas, and had begun a strong military offensive that was in the process of defeating the most select army units. Batista's days were clearly numbered.

The clandestine struggle was growing in the cities. The three organizations that made up the Revolutionary Front — the July 26 Movement, the Popular Socialist Party and the Revolutionary Directorate — stepped up the sabotage, strikes and other civil actions, bringing to their feet the entire population which, for the first time in its neocolonial history, was nearing the moment of emancipation.

It was precisely in those days that an interesting meeting was held in the general headquarters of the armed forces of the Dominican Republic with the dictator Rafael Leónidas Trujillo, another U.S. protégé who spoke with great concern to his most trusted generals about the events in the neighboring country: Castro will surely overthrow Batista and then what will be his next step? he asked. Will he spread his revolution throughout the Caribbean? In that case, how could the Dominican Army resist such well-trained guerrillas? Shouldn't the Dominican Republic perhaps have, as do Spain and France, a foreign legion, a body of mercenaries who work for hire?

The interlocutors agreed with him; they all understood the dangers that could come with the triumph of a people's revolution in Cuba. They knew of the help given to Batista and of the sympathies that the Cuban rebels were awakening in their own people. It was essential to keep the example from spreading to Dominicans. They were sure that the United States would support them, since it also had the same concerns. Trujillo took charge of the operation. He recruited a mercenary army to seize the power from the revolutionary Cubans, should they happen to take it.[9] Perhaps Batista could not return, but there would be no lack of men to head a government which would calm the fiery spirits of the Cubans.

But it was already too late. The advance of the revolutionary forces was unstoppable. On December 31, 1958, while Trujillo celebrated the New Year and reviewed his plans which when put into action would make him the standard-bearer of anti-communism, Batista and his closest accomplices came knocking on his door, asking for asylum. The dictatorship had fallen.

---

[9] "Testimony of a traveler arriving from Santo Domingo." *Hoy*, August 1, 1959.

CHAPTER 2

The Trujillo conspiracy

On January 1, 1959, Fidel Castro and his Rebel Army victoriously entered Santiago de Cuba, the island's second largest city, after defeating the best units of Batista's army. The public gave them a glorious welcome. A coup was attempted in Havana to stop them from consolidating their victory. However, Fidel Castro's call for a general strike and the massive response of the whole nation foiled the maneuver.

The following day, during a meeting in the general headquarters of the armed forces of the Dominican Republic, Trujillo again spoke about creating a "foreign legion," and the first plans against Cuba began to take shape.[10] Between January and March of that year, several hundred mercenaries were recruited and secretly transferred to the Dominican Republic at a cost of millions of dollars. Two hundred former Batista soldiers were incorporated into the force.

The CIA knew about the plans and reported them to the highest levels of the U.S. government. Richard Nixon, then Vice-President of the United States, was interested in the details and gave the Agency the green light to send a senior official to meet with Trujillo and evaluate the seriousness of the anti-Cuba project. This man was known as Gerry Droller (with the aliases

---

[10] "Vida, pasión y muerte de una conspiración." An exclusive report in the "En Cuba" section of *Bohemia*, August 23, 1959.

Frank Bender or Don Federico), a German who had served as a U.S. agent during the Second World War.

In Florida, the former soldiers of Batista's army began organizing, and they were quickly joined by old politicians and new capitalist and pseudorevolutionary immigrants who had wanted the revolution to reestablish "democracy." These were the backbone of the first counterrevolutionary organization founded in the United States for the purpose of overthrowing the Cuban government. They hypocritically called themselves the White Rose, after Martí's poem, and claimed to represent the tradition of the national independence hero José Martí.

They planned to capitalize on the favors of the U.S. government to recover the power they had lost in Cuba. In short, those who never defended the country when they ran it wanted to get it back with the help of Uncle Sam. That is how they ended up in the arms of their only possible ally: the dictator Trujillo, who saw this as the instrument for organizing both a fifth column and external support which would facilitate the mercenary invasion by his new foreign legion.

Meanwhile, in Cuba, in early 1959, an expedition of revolutionary Dominicans and Cubans organized and landed on Quisqueyan soil. The Trujillo dictatorship inspired such condemnation that young people from throughout Latin America lent their support to their sister nation's struggle. Secretly, the U.S. embassy — which was aware of the plans — supplied some resources for the enterprise through its agents Frank Sturgis and Gerry Hemming at the same time that it was working on the details for facilitating Trujillo's projected disembarkation. In reality, the idea was to manipulate the revolutionaries in order to enable Trujillo's planned aggression to take place.

The idea of seizing this opportunity and using it in the aggression against Cuba was approved by the dictator. He sent ambassadors to Washington and other capitals on the American continent to call a meeting of the Organization of American States (OAS) to accuse the revolutionary Cuban government of interfering in the internal affairs of the Dominican Republic, creating an excuse for the military aggression that was being planned. Cuba was charged with "exporting revolution." Perhaps that was the first time this accusation was leveled against the Cuban government — a fallacy which would later be wielded against Cuba by the United States and numerous other Latin American dictatorships.

Several months before the alleged Cuban meddling, toward the end of February 1959, CIA representative Frank Bender met with Trujillo and his chief of intelligence Colonel Johnny Abbes García to analyze the plans that they were preparing against Cuba. Bender considered that the Caribbean Legion — as the mercenary expedition was to be called — could be converted into a kind of police force to be used whenever necessary. In actual fact, the plans were already well under way and the United States didn't even have to give its public consent. It only had to look the other way and then, once the deed was done, pretend that it had just heard about it. In other words, once again the United States could plausibly deny any involvement.

Bender's only recommendation was to send emissaries to Cuba to recruit renegades and enhance the idea that in Cuba there was opposition among the revolutionary forces themselves. But he failed to mention that he already had agents in place doing just that, among them William Morgan.

Morgan had received his rank of commander in the Second Front of the Escambray, and after January 1 he was assigned some military responsibilities — but he was so undisciplined that he was soon relieved of them and placed in the reserves. His wounded feelings got the better of him and he began to seek out the company of other officials of the Second Front in the same circumstances. His colleague John Spiritto had killed a Rebel Army sergeant in a brawl and was now a fugitive. Both of them felt cheated because they did not receive the cushy positions they had expected.

In mid-February, a meeting took place between Spiritto and his case officer, the "diplomat" Arthur Avignon, who informed him that the CIA station had decided to provisionally suspend its contacts with him. In the coming weeks an emissary would arrive from abroad with new instructions.

During the first days of March, Morgan received a telephone call from a U.S. mafioso named Fred Nelson. He was Trujillo's messenger. A meeting then took place in a room in Havana's Hotel Capri. After hours of conversation and a few drinks too many, Morgan declared emphatically that for a million dollars he would turn the Second Front against the revolution and "bounce Fidel Castro from power!" The next day Nelson called to see if, sober, Morgan would stand by his offer. After receiving a reassurance, Nelson advised him that if he accepted the proposal he would have to travel to Miami to concretize the plans with the Dominican consul there.

On March 12, 1959, Fred Nelson arrived in the Dominican Republic to inform Trujillo of the deal he had made with Morgan and the possibility it presented of showing that it was the rebels themselves who wanted to get rid of Castro. It was agreed that Morgan would receive his million dollars. Half would be deposited in a bank account, and he would get the rest when he completed the operation.

Only a few weeks later, in mid-April, Fidel Castro made his first official visit to the United States and met with Vice-President Richard Nixon. In this meeting he explained in detail the perspectives of the revolution. After Fidel left, Nixon wrote a memorandum to President Dwight D. Eisenhower, assuring him that the Cuban leader was a confirmed communist and should be removed from power.

Almost simultaneously, on April 15, Morgan traveled to Miami and made contact in a hotel room at the Du Pont Plaza with Colonel Augusto Ferrando, the Dominican consul in that city. Also present were the arms dealer Fred Boscher and the counterrevolutionary Manuel Benítez. They explained the plans to invade Cuba with a foreign legion under the command of José Eluterio Pedraza, a general in Batista's army; and the need to organize an internal uprising as a prelude to the aggression. They expressed their belief that the Second Front and the White Rose counterrevolutionary group could carry out this task. The White Rose was composed of various isolated cells throughout the island, mainly ex-soldiers of the Batista regime, under the command of the former *casquitos* Renaldo Blanco Navarro and Claudio Medel. Another nucleus of the conspiracy, formed by members of those classes displaced from power, was led by Dr. Armando Caíñas Milanés, president of the Ranchers Association of Cuba.

The topic of reimbursement took up more of the discussion than the plans themselves. The final agreement was that Pedraza would get half a million dollars at the time of the invasion and the other half would be placed in a bank account.

A week later Morgan returned to Miami to report on the progress of the conspiracy. He explained that Eloy Gutiérrez Menoyo, together with the most important leaders of the organization, had agreed to participate in the plot, but only on the condition that the U.S. government supported it. Colonel Ferrando told them that it was coordinated at the highest levels of government, and gave Gutiérrez Menoyo the necessary assurances. The money for operating expenses would be distributed in $10,000 installments to two of Morgan's emissaries who traveled to Miami periodically.

When John Spiritto learned of the plans in which Morgan and Gutiérrez Menoyo were involved, he tried to reestablish contact with his case officer. The latter, however, refused to meet with him. The embassy had undergone profound changes with the appointment of Ambassador Philip Bonsal, a seasoned diplomat who, in an effort to erase the proconsul image of his predecessor, had placed a number of obstacles to running CIA activities out of the embassy because this threatened to affect diplomatic relations.

The trips by Morgan and Gutiérrez Menoyo to Florida began to arouse such suspicion that the Information Department of the Rebel Army (G-2) was alerted to their planned treason. The conspirators feared that Fidel Castro was already aware of their plans. Once again demonstrating his two-faced nature, Gutiérrez Menoyo suggested to Morgan that they inform the leader of the revolution. They agreed not to mention the money they had received, much less the extent of the plans, so that when the moment came they could have all the cards in their hands. If the legion landed in Cuba and consolidated its positions, they could again switch sides.

The next day Gutiérrez Menoyo went to the Presidential Palace to ask for an urgent secret meeting with Fidel Castro. The meeting took place in an apartment on 11th Street in the Vedado neighborhood. Gutiérrez Menoyo and Morgan reported on the conspiracy, justifying their initial silence on the pretext that they had waited to see "how serious" the plans really were. They explained that the Trinidad area had been selected as the site where the mercenaries would land. The spurs of the Escambray mountains were the ideal place to establish the provisional government that would accompany the legion. Morgan and his accomplices were expected to arrange uprisings in the nearby mountains and, at the appointed time, cut communications and ambush the troops on their way to stop the invasion.

Fidel listened patiently and finally authorized them to continue, while instructions were given to the security agencies to penetrate the conspiracy. The period which would really test the Cuban intelligence capabilities and the revolution's capacity to respond to subversion had begun.

For the purpose of coordinating the activities, the Dominican intelligence services sent three Viking Valiant radio trans-mitters with 20 meter directional antennas and other necessary equipment. In Miami, those responsible for purchasing arms were Trujillo's son-in-law, Porfirio Rubiroso, a Don Juan in the gambling casinos, and the Cuban mercenary Félix Bernardino. They received a "donation" of $200,000 from the former Venezuelan dictator Marcos Pérez Jiménez, who wanted to win the favor of his Dominican colleague in the hope that it might help return him to power having been deposed a year earlier by a revolution.

While all this was going on, Fidel was receiving constant information about the movements of the enemy. By mid-July the revolutionary leadership was familiar with the main elements of the conspiracy. These included provoking an uprising in the Escambray by the forces of the Second Front; and having men from Batista's army, who now served the Revolutionary Armed

Forces as instructors and technicians, seize the tanks and heavy artillery and sabotage the few planes belonging to the Cuban Air Force. When the Trujillo troops bombed the installations of the Rebel Army, it would be unable to defend itself.

In the hours following these actions, the foreign legion, with a force of some 3,000 men, would land on a beach known as El Inglés, in southern Las Villas Province, between Cienfuegos and Trinidad. A wave of sabotage and assassinations would be unleashed in Havana and other cities to convince international public opinion that chaos and anarchy reigned in Cuba and thus justify the legionnaires' invasion. The United States would take advantage of this to denounce the deteriorating Cuban-Dominican conflict and the alleged violations of human rights on the island at an OAS meeting in Chile called by Trujillo, setting the stage to request that the OAS carry out an urgent collective intervention in order to "pacify the Cuban upheaval."

In early July, an emissary of Trujillo, a Spanish priest named Ricardo Velazco Ordóñez, arrived in Havana. Under his cassock he carried instructions to review the preparations for Morgan and Gutiérrez Menoyo's uprising, put them in contact with other counterrevolutionary groups, and coordinate their activities. He was given a chauffeur who would also serve as his bodyguard.

After meeting with several of the conspirators, his chauffeur eagerly drove him to meet with former Senator Arturo Hernández Tellaheche and Dr. Caíñas Milanés. In the name of Trujillo, he offered them the presidency and vice-presidency of the future administration. After the proper genuflection, they both accepted. Ramón Mestre Gutiérrez, the former owner of the Naroca Construction Company would be named prime minister and the minister of government was to be the well-known turncoat Rolando Masferrer. That mix of "political personalities" was completely acceptable to all.

Father Velazco left the meeting satisfied. He reclined comfortably in the passenger seat of his automobile, and in all probability he dreamed that night of the success of his venture. On July 20, accompanied as usual by his bodyguard, he left for his last meeting in the Hotel Capri. Also at the meeting were

Morgan, Hernández Tellaheche, Mestre and other co-conspirators. There they placed the final touches on the plans and set a tentative date for smuggling arms into Cuba for use by the counterrevolutionaries. When the priest bid a grateful goodbye to his chauffeur at the airport, he had no way of knowing that the man who had accompanied him everywhere for nearly a month was a Cuban G-2 agent.

On July 28, Morgan again visited Miami. There he received a boatload of arms from the Dominican consul, part of which he was to deliver to the San Felipe and Los Indios Keys, near the Isle of Pines in Cuba. The rest was to be put ashore near Trinidad, to supply the guerrilla groups in the region.

Meanwhile, preparations were underway to liquidate the conspiracy and Gutiérrez Menoyo began to "cooperate" to a greater extent. In his later meetings with Fidel Castro, he had demonstrated that he knew all the details of Trujillo's plans. The G-2 had decisively infiltrated the ranks of the agents, not only those close to Morgan, but also those close to Trujillo. Gutiérrez Menoyo understood this. His only alternative was to use his chameleonic talents to change color once again and help to dismantle the conspiracy. He had taken advantage of the absence of his associate to report some details that he had "forgotten" in the whirlwind of events.

The signal to set off the counter plan would be given by Morgan himself, without his knowing it, when he reported to Havana that he was headed for the island with the arms shipment. At that moment the roundup of the conspirators began, dismantling the fifth column that was to have facilitated the invasion and capturing the men and weapons of the foreign legion.

On August 6, Morgan weighed anchor in Florida with the weapons on board, but bad weather obliged him to alter his course. On August 8, at 12:30 a.m., he docked his yacht at a tiny pier in Regla in Havana Bay. At dawn the same day, Fidel inspected the booty: an entire arsenal which included forty 30 caliber machine guns, dozens of rifles and a large quantity of ammunition.

The foreign legion was due to land in the next 72 hours. Morgan and Gutiérrez Menoyo were transferred to the Escambray as scheduled. There, accompanied by Commander Camilo Cienfuegos and other Cuban officials, they moved to El Inglés Beach, near Trinidad. Meanwhile, the plotters were housed in various homes, waiting for news. This enabled the capture that night of nearly a thousand counterrevolutionaries. The following day a group of 24 of Batista's former *casquitos* were also apprehended when they tried to rise up in arms in the vicinity of the Soledad Sugar Mill, east of the city of Cienfuegos.

Radio equipment was set up in the Escambray. Gutiérrez Menoyo communicated with Trujillo and the following dialogue ensued.

"3JK calling KJB."

"3JK come in please. KJB here. I hear you loud and clear."

"Instructions completed. I am now in the mountains fighting the communists. The American landed at the appointed spot. Now everything is in your hands. *Viva Cuba libre!*"

This transmission was confirmed by UPI, which reported on the uprisings against the revolutionary government.

At his headquarters, General Trujillo couldn't contain his delight, since his plans seemed to be marching full steam ahead. What Trujillo didn't know was that both the transmission and the press release originated at the headquarters of the Cuban government.

On the same day, August 8, in Havana, Cuban State Security arrested two U.S. embassy officials. One of them was Sgt. Stanley F. Wesson, who was officially accredited as a member of the security service of the embassy. He was detained while directing a meeting of counterrevolutionary elements to carry out sabotage and other actions in support of Trujillo's plans.

On Sunday night, August 9, a Dominican Air Force plane flew over the Escambray mountain range. At the tiny rustic airport in El Nicho, government troops illuminated the runway, but weather conditions impeded the landing and the aircraft returned to its base. At approximately 10:00 the next morning, Morgan established communication with Colonel Abbes, informing him of the advance of the troops of the Second Front. According to the disinformation in the report, they controlled a vast area and were preparing to take the city of Trinidad.

The Voz Dominicana radio station broadcast constant messages of encouragement to the counterrevolutionaries, who they believed were on the verge of taking power. At exactly 2:00 a.m. on Tuesday, August 11, the combatants posted on El Inglés Beach heard the humming of the motors of a transport plane. The highway of the southern circuit was lit up with multicolored lights which the pilot could see from high above. Minutes later several parachutes with military supplies were dropped over the mountains and the nearby beach, where they were recovered shortly after dawn. Santo Domingo received a report of the successful operation and the imminent capture of the city of Trinidad. After a detailed analysis of the evolution of events, Fidel decided to expand the theater of military operations and to feign the capture of Trinidad by the counterrevolutionaries. With this maneuver the enemy would gain confidence and dispatch more arms shipments and finally send their "famous" foreign legion into combat.

The international press agencies, alerted by confidential sources, began to report some of the arrests and this caused Trujillo to mistrust the plan and stop sending aircraft. That night the "plotters" communicated with the Dominican dictator who requested that Morgan come to the transmitter.

"3JK. KJB here, over."

"The American speaking," responded Morgan.

"What's going on!" shouted the dictator. "The news arriving here is disastrous. They say everybody's been captured and you're about to be captured too. What can you tell me? Over."

"The news from the press agencies is being fabricated by the government. You know those people are experts in propaganda. It's a plan to create confusion and avoid the reinforcements that they imagine are on the way."

Morgan stepped back from the microphone, a signal for Fidel, who was listening to the communication. He came closer and murmured in a low voice.

"3JK calling KJB."

"Go ahead, 3JK."

"I have just been informed that Trinidad has fallen to our troops. You can now send the shipments to the airport."

That same night, August 11, the Rebel Army forces occupied Trinidad and shut off the electricity, explaining to the population the reason for the measures being taken.

The next day, after a flurry of messages in both directions, it was agreed that another plane would be sent with Trujillo's personal emissary aboard. At approximately 7:00 in the evening a C-47 transport plane flew over the airport. Minutes later it landed quickly and stopped in the middle of the runway without shutting down its motors. When the door of the plane opened, out stepped the familiar pudgy figure of Father Velazco, who was immediately greeted by shouts of "Viva Trujillo!" Soldiers disguised as peasants created the illusion of popular support. The priest, moved, saluted from the staircase to several officials who applauded him. A short distance away, the scene of machine guns and artillery shells gave the impression that a fierce combat had taken place the night before.

Totally convinced, Velazco parted with the promise to send more arms and well-trained personnel. Hours later he gave his report to the Dominican dictator who, posturing as a Roman tribune, pronounced the fall of Fidel Castro and authorized the flights to continue according to the original plans.

On the morning of August 13, by order of Fidel, the radio team sent a message to Santo Domingo: "The troops of the Second Front advanced on Manicaragua and later fell on Santa Clara. A counterattack by Fidel's forces has retaken the Soledad Sugar Mill, but Rio Hondo, Cumanayagua, El Salto and Caonao continue to be under our control. We must take advantage of the state of demoralization to land our foreign legion which will give them the final kick."

The news was so encouraging that Trujillo thought that using the foreign legion would be unnecessary, thus saving several million dollars. Perhaps he thought to himself, "Once Santa Clara is in the hands of the counterrevolutionaries, I'll send a small symbolic force." Following this strategy, he ordered that a message be sent to Morgan explaining that the legion would be dispatched when conditions were more favorable, but that in the meantime he would send another plane with military supplies, advisers, and a personal emissary with new instructions.

It was evident that the foreign legion was not coming. Therefore, the revolutionary leadership decided to end the game after capturing the aircraft. They already had sufficient evidence of the Trujillo conspiracy. At around 8:00 p.m. another C-47 flew over Trinidad. Aboard was Lieutenant Colonel Antonio Soto Rodríguez, pilot of the plane in which Batista had fled from Cuba, and Carlos Vals, the copilot. The special envoy sent by Trujillo to meet with Morgan and Gutiérrez Menoyo and to inspect the fighting at the front was Luis Del Pozo, son of the mayor of Havana during the Batista dictatorship. The other passengers were former Captain Francisco Betancourt, a fugitive from revolutionary justice; Roberto Martín Pérez, son of a well-known constable; Pedro Rivero Moreno, ex-*casquito* and fugitive from justice; Alfredo Malibrán Moreno, a Spanish mercenary and specialist in bazookas; and Raúl Díaz Prieto, Armando Valera Salgado, Raúl Carvajal Hernández and Sigfredo Rodríguez Díaz. Six of them planned to stay, and the others were going to return to Santo Domingo.

Fifteen minutes later the plane landed. The party descended and, to the astonishment of everyone present, Del Pozo warmly embraced Gutiérrez Menoyo. They were old friends. "I come as Trujillo's personal envoy," Luis Del Pozo announced. "I bring all of you greetings in his name." He immediately asked for a map with the positions to be bombarded by the Dominican Air Force marked on it, and inquired as to the number of legionnaires needed for the final actions.

After this brief conversation, everyone headed toward the airport installations. It was the signal. The militia who were unloading the boxes of arms and ammunition sprang into action. The mercenaries found themselves staring into gun barrels. The copilot opened fire and a gun battle ensued which lasted more than 10 minutes. Two revolutionaries and two legionnaires were killed. The others were arrested. Important documents with information about plots in other parts of the country were found in their possession. An amusing anecdote is that when Luis Del Pozo, Trujillo's special envoy, found himself surprised by the revolutionary troops, he fainted.

On August 14, Fidel Castro appeared before the national television cameras and revealed the entire saga of the international conspiracy. On that occasion he remarked, "Trujillo is a freelance gangster, supported by the OAS."

Thus ended the Trujillo conspiracy, the first major attempt to overthrow the Cuban revolution, which had all the classic characteristics of a CIA operation: internal insurrection, destabilization and mercenary invasion linked to an OAS maneuver with the complicity of the traditional allies of the United States in order to lend legitimacy to a military intervention with the "altruistic purpose" of pacifying the island.

A short time later the chameleons Eloy Gutiérrez Menoyo and William Morgan again changed their uniforms. In November 1960, Morgan was arrested as he tried to organize — for the CIA — a band of counterrevolutionaries in the Escambray mountains for the purpose of providing support for an invasion that was planned in the following months. In January 1961, Gutiérrez Menoyo deserted to the United States to work for his masters there and participate in the "new government" that the United States was planning to place in power in Cuba.

CHAPTER 3

The plot

The Agrarian Reform Law, proclaimed by the revolutionary government on May 17, 1959, was a warning to Cuban and U.S. capital that the revolution had begun to expand its measures to the benefit of the Cuban people. As an inevitable consequence, a new type of opposition emerged, representing segments of the upper and middle classes, transnational corporations and the Catholic hierarchy, joined by deserters from the revolutionary ranks, those who only aspired to overthrow the dictator in order to get their own hands on the spoils of office.

The first steps taken by this opposition were aimed at pressuring revolutionary authorities to put the brakes on, or at least moderate the social program being carried out. Political events were unfolding rapidly and there was an overwhelming response to every attempt to stop the social reforms. Soon the opposition, under the protection of the U.S. embassy, took upon itself the task of trying to halt the revolutionary process.

The Catholic hierarchy was particularly active. Its churches were used to distribute propaganda and lay organizations emerged with political structures which sought to challenge the influence of the revolution in work centers and intellectual and student circles.

The United States government, encouraged by the economic interests who saw their privileges on the island threatened, called a secret meeting during the month of May 1959. Those present included Vice-President Richard Nixon, Ambassador William Pawley, an adviser to President Dwight D. Eisenhower, senior executives of Pepsi Cola International, Esso, Standard Oil, the United Fruit Company and of course representatives of the Mafia. They made a pact in which Nixon promised to overthrow the Cuban government in exchange for their support for his candidacy in the upcoming presidential election.[11]

Between May and June of that year, the Social Christian Party was founded in Cuba. It was headed by a professor at the Villanueva Catholic University, José Ignacio Rasco. This organization hoped to become a political force in the name of the "vital classes" of society which could contain the avalanche of revolutionary measures. Rasco's political evolution had begun years before in 1957 when he founded — together with other "prominent" individuals — a tiny party called the Radical Liberal Party, which was intended to become a political alternative to the Batista dictatorship. The strategy was clear: from a position of legality, use the Social Christian Party to exert pressure, while the religious, fraternal and social organizations acted to create a climate of opposition, discontent and fear. In that way they

---

[11] Richard Nixon, *Six crises* (New York: Doubleday), 352. In this book Nixon admits that after his meeting in Washington with Fidel Castro in April 1959, he proposed dealing with Castro without any illusions that he would submit to the dictates of the United States, a criteria shared by Arthur Gardner and Earl T. Smith, former U.S. ambassadors in Havana, as well as William Pawley. He admitted that in 1960 he gave instructions to the CIA to supply weapons, ammunition and training to Cubans who had fled from the "Castro regime" and were living in exile in the United States and various Latin American countries. "This program had been in operation for six months before the 1960 [presidential] campaign got under way," Nixon wrote. "It was a program, however, that I could say not one word about. The operation was covert. Under no circumstances could it be disclosed or even alluded to. Consequently, under Kennedy's attacks and his new demands for 'militant' policies, I was in a position of a fighter with one hand tied behind his back. I knew we had a program under way to deal with Castro, but I could not even hint at its existence, much less spell it out."

aspired to impose a socio-political program on the revolutionary government which would change its course.

Slowly the conspiracy began to be implemented. Humberto Sorí Marín, Huber Matos Benítez and Manuel Artime Buesa were among those selected to lead this new opposition. Among the documents captured from Trujillo's "invaders" was a very interesting letter. In part, it read: "Huber Matos is a man of the right, a Doctor of Pedagogy, and an accommodating person with ample economic resources and cordial relations with the great ranching and sugarcane interests in Camagüey." In fact, Matos, Sorí Marín, and Artime had many interests in common. The three came from wealthy backgrounds and were linked to Cuban capital and the traditional politicians.

Huber Matos joined the rebel forces during the first half of 1958, when he arrived in the Sierra Maestra as part of an air expedition bringing arms and ammunition acquired by the July 26 Movement in Costa Rica. He soon stood out as an ambitious and undisciplined person whom Fidel Castro himself had to reprimand on more than one occasion. At the end of the war, his egotism and visceral anticommunism set him up as the enemy incarnate of the revolution, a "merit" which helped to promote him as a political leader of the landholders, the bourgeoisie and the reactionary clergy in the southern part of Oriente Province.

Humberto Sorí Marín also joined the rebels in the Sierra Maestra, where he subsequently became a commander of the Rebel Army. At the triumph of the revolution, he participated in the first administration as Minister of Agriculture, with the job of promoting the agrarian reform announced in the Moncada platform. Long conversations with representatives of the U.S. embassy's Agricultural Development Program — called "Point IV" — convinced him of the advantages of retaining private ownership of the land, except for that which had belonged to the closest collaborators of the Batista regime. That way there could be "agrarian reform" of sorts and some peasants could benefit without affecting other major interests.

Sorí Marín appointed numerous directors of agricultural development in different eastern regions. His goal was to place men he could trust in key positions and thus control relations with the sharecroppers and squatters. This would increase internal conflicts and could undermine their support for the revolution.

Among those he appointed was Manuel Artime Buesa, in zone number 022 of the eastern region of Manzanillo. Artime had a certain theatrical manner. He was a founder, along with Rasco, of the Radical Liberal Party and had the foresight to go into the Sierra Maestra some 72 hours before the triumph of the revolution. He obtained the rank of lieutenant thanks to his friendship with Sorí Marín and he gained recognition in the early months of 1959 as a virulent anticommunist when he published *Comunismo ¿para qué?* [Communism, what for?], designed to disorient and divide the revolutionary movement. In Manzanillo, Artime organized some rural commandos, with the support of the Catholic University Association (ACU), on the pretext of teaching literacy to the peasants, but with the intention of influencing and using them for his own objectives.

Toward the middle of the year, seeing his plans frustrated, Sorí Marín resigned from his post and joined the conspiracy. Ever present in this unfolding counterrevolutionary drama were the old followers of Carlos Prío, Tony Varona, Aureliano Sánchez Arango and other members of the *Auténticos*, who aspired to regain the power they had lost with Batista's military coup. Sorí Marín and Manuel Artime elaborated a plan, with the support of Prío, Varona and Sánchez Arango, to organize subversion in the eastern part of the country. They planned an uprising of a detachment of men in the Manzanillo area under Artime's command. Once that area was up in arms, they would land weapons and military supplies, allowing them to consolidate this base, which they expected to quickly spread to the rest of the country.

Meanwhile, the aristocratic mansions of Havana were the scene of intense meetings, which were frequently honored by the presence of U.S. embassy officials. The obligatory topic was the marked "communist tendency" of the government, attributed to Raúl Castro and Che Guevara, the principal instigators — so they said — of the popular measures that were being taken. Communist infiltration was seen as the cause of the great social upheavals on the island, as if misery, illiteracy, disease and dictatorship were of no consequence.

The ideological campaigns began to bear fruit. Hundreds of professionals and other persons from the middle class, together with the politicians who had returned to the country following the revolution in search of their old privileged positions, emigrated to the United States. They sought the protection of the empire until things settled down. There they organized an intensive propaganda campaign denouncing "the dangers of communism in Cuba." The objective was to launch a political and military movement to which other forces could be added to destabilize the revolutionary government, eliminate its leaders, and reverse the popular measures. There was a clear connection between the plans for the counterrevolutionary emigration and the internal conspiracies. The hand of the CIA was behind both of them.

Huber Matos, aware of the plans, offered to instigate the Camagüey Regiment to revolt, where he had carried out patient work, weeding out those officers who didn't share his views and placing his followers in all of the principal positions of command. He could also count on some provincial officials and some of the mass media. In that way, his pronouncement would be made public, and the government would have no other alternative — he thought — than to negotiate with him.

In the first days of the month of September, a social gathering was held at the home of a well-known member of the Havana bourgeoisie.[12] A number of "friends" were invited, including the First Secretary of the U.S. embassy, Edward C. Wilson, Humberto Sorí Marín, Huber Matos, and Manuel Artime. They sipped cocktails and commented on current political issues. The relaxed atmosphere of the "party" promoted the formation of clusters of various like-minded persons who casually discussed the latest political news.

---

[12] Report from Cuban State Security. September 1959.

Sorí Marín, Matos, and Artime retired to a back room in the house. They sat there comfortably and the conversation continued. Matos described the situation in the country as "unbearable." "If we don't isolate the communists from the government and the command of troops, it will be the end of us. You've already seen how Fidel liquidated Urrutia and his new ministers in order to impose the Agrarian Reform Law, which is more communist than the one the Russians implemented," he concluded.

"We shouldn't act precipitously," responded Sorí Marín. "The Americans have asked us for a little patience. Fidel still has significant popular support and many people are excited about the social measures taken by the government. We should think carefully about what we are going to do. Artime has done magnificent political work in southern Oriente and there are other military commands that we can count on, when the moment arrives. Besides, all the businessmen are on our side. I'm only worried about whether the people will go out into the streets to defend Fidel and this will turn into a bloodbath. If the Americans were to make some declaration condemning the government, perhaps that would be the opportune moment. It should be clear to everyone that without the United States we would die of hunger."

The silence that followed Sorí Marín's last words enabled the others to reflect for a moment. It was true, a clear stance taken by the United States would clear up much of the indecision. Besides, who would have dreamed that Cuba could exist without the support of its neighbor to the north? Artime took advantage of the occasion suggesting, "We have to make our decision before the Americans. The appropriate thing to do is to launch a rebel movement and give the United States sufficient motivation to assume a belligerent position toward Castro. In this way, when relations are broken between the two countries we will be in a very advantageous position. Then nobody can dispute our strength and we will be the ones selected to form the new government, organize the next elections, and then. . ."

They each defined their views during that conversation, and their actions followed accordingly. A few weeks earlier the head of the Air Force, Pedro Luis Díaz Lanz had deserted, and within a few days he had joined his old friend Frank Sturgis. They marched off together into exile to form a counterrevolutionary organization which they preached would "rescue the true ideals of the Cuban revolution."

There was no doubt that the U.S. embassy pulled the strings of the conspiracy that was slowly taking shape. The new chief of the CIA station, James Noel, had a team of almost 30 officials with which to recruit and train counterrevolutionaries. The link with Artime was Bernard Baker, an old police official of the Batista dictatorship and future Watergate "plumber." Baker was a U.S. citizen of Cuban origin who after participating in World War II returned to Cuba to act as a spy within the police force. Through this conduit, Artime kept the embassy informed about developments.

A great political battle was looming: the elections at the University of Havana. "The Hill," as this center of higher learning is affectionately called, had historically been a bastion of revolutionary ideas. Many of the young people who attacked the dictator in his den at the Presidential Palace on March 13, 1957, came from the university; and before that it had been the cradle of a series of political movements which challenged each new dictatorship.

The elections were set for October 18, 1959, and the reactionaries, the bourgeoisie and the clergy chose the university as the stage where they could take the pulse of the revolution. The Catholic University Association was supported by the representatives of Prío and Varona in running Pedro Luis Boitel as their candidate for the presidency of the FEU (Federation of University Students). Boitel was a cadre from their ranks who had carried out an intensely divisive campaign, branding all of the revolutionaries who did not share his point of view as "communist infiltrators." The political struggle heated up, and soon the reactionaries were unmasked. The revolutionary candidates won the elections, demonstrating that the Cuban students unconditionally supported those who stood for the ideals of the Julio Antonio Mella and José Antonio Echeverría, martyrs from the university.

However, events were accelerating. The following day, October 19, Huber Matos, head of the Rebel Army regiment in Camagüey Province, gathered his men around him and publicly resigned, on the pretext of "communists" dominating the government. His plan consisted of calling for a general strike in the region, with the help of his followers. At that time a convention on international tourism was being held in the capital which had attracted hundreds of delegates and journalists from all over the world. They were to be the witnesses who would report on the public reaction to the actions.

A revolutionary response was organized rapidly. Fidel ordered Captain Jorge Enrique Mendoza, head of the National Institute for Agrarian Reform (INRA) in Camagüey, to occupy all the positions with police forces, take control of the telegraph office and the airport, and assume combat positions around the city. At the same time he ordered Commander Camilo Cienfuegos, head of the Rebel Army, to go to Camagüey to make the rebellious forces surrender. His audacity overwhelmed the seditionists. Camilo arrived at the barracks and after a heated confrontation he was able to force Huber Matos and the other officials involved in the conspiracy to surrender, and to persuade those who were confused of the true intentions of the plotters. Hours later Fidel himself went to the provincial capital where at an impressive show of support for the revolution, he unmasked the counterrevolutionary plot.

On October 21, Pedro Luis Díaz Lanz and Frank Sturgis, flying a CIA plane, scattered thousands of leaflets over the city of Havana, exhorting the population to rise up against the revolution. Two days later Manuel Artime circulated an open letter to Fidel in which he resigned his position with the INRA in Manzanillo and accused Fidel of having surrendered to "international communism." Artime took advantage of the occasion to abscond with more than a hundred thousand pesos of funds under his control and take refuge in a Latin American embassy while awaiting an opportunity to flee the country. From his hiding place he sent an urgent message for help to James Noel, CIA chief at the U.S. embassy, who ordered Bernard Baker to activate his contacts to spirit the embezzler off the island. A few days later, Artime was surreptitiously moved to a ship flying a Honduran flag anchored in the Havana Bay, which rapidly turned its prow northward.

On October 28, after defeating the revolt in Camagüey, while returning to Havana in an Armed Forces plane, Camilo Cienfuegos, commander of a thousand battles, died in a tragic accident. All Cuba was dressed in mourning. One of the commanders of the Sierra had fallen, the hero who, together with Che Guevara, repeated the historic east-to-west invasion of Antonio Maceo during the Independence War. Camilo was a man with a broad smile to whom words came easily and who, upon receiving his rank of commander, wrote to Fidel saying, "It would be easier for me to stop breathing than to betray your confidence."

The arrest of Huber Matos put an end to the attempt to change the direction of the revolution through the use of renegade forces, and so the counterrevolution began to move abroad, placing its leadership in the undisputed hands of the hawks of the CIA.

CHAPTER 4

Operation 40

*Covert action is activity which is meant to further the
sponsoring nation's foreign policy objectives, and to be
concealed in order to permit that nation to
plausibly deny responsibility.*[13]

The CIA was created in 1947 to do the dirty work of U.S.
foreign policy, and the National Security Council
immediately issued a decree giving it authority to conduct
covert operations. The law which formally created the Central
Intelligence Agency did not in fact give it autonomy for covert
actions, but rather established a National Security Council under
the control of the U.S. President, to evaluate and approve all
covert operations, as well as the Agency's budget. Nevertheless, at
its very first meeting, this council gave the CIA the necessary
authority to carry out covert actions.

In reality, the policy of plausible deniability is as old as the
United States itself. It has been applied to all the political and
military interventions carried out on our continent during the
past hundred years.

When the United States government decided to overthrow
the Cuban revolution, the job was turned over to the CIA, in this
case with the blessing of all the "saints" in Washington. There

---

[13] *Alleged assassination plots,* 9.

were a great many economic interests behind this decision. William Pawley, who had been U.S. ambassador to Brazil and Peru and who owned the gas company in Havana and was an intimate friend of the executives of the United Fruit Company, was President Eisenhower's adviser on Cuban affairs. Colonel J.C. King, chief of the Western Hemisphere Division of the CIA, was an associate of Pawley and also had important interests on the island.

There was also the business of the Mafia. Meyer Lansky, Santos Trafficante, Joe Colombo and other capos had large investments in Cuba, principally in gambling and prostitution, both of which were eradicated after the 1959 revolution. It is easy to comprehend why this unholy alliance formed so rapidly to halt the political process that had begun to germinate on the neighboring island, the former emporium of vice and corruption exported by the United States.

In late November 1959, James Noel, CIA station chief in Havana, met with his closest collaborator to analyze the evolution of the political situation in Cuba. He had received instructions from Colonel King to prepare this analysis. His years with the Agency had taught him that when his boss personally asked for a report, big issues were involved and since nobody could swim against the current, he took great care. He believed that there were still individuals in the Cuban government that could be won over to the cause of the United States; that everything had not ended with the capture of Huber Matos and his associates; and that men such as Sorí Marín had definite influence. However, he knew he should be cautious when offering his opinions, since an error could cost him his career. Therefore he adopted a dual position, giving King the report that he wanted to hear, while at the same time — with his pawns — he continued playing the game. The document that the CIA specialists drafted concluded:

> Fidel Castro, under the influence of his closest collaborators, particularly his brother Raúl and Che Guevara, has been converted to communism. Cuba is preparing to export its

revolution to other countries of the hemisphere and spread the war against capitalism.[14]

With these words, they pronounced a death sentence for the Cuban revolution. Days later, on December 11, Colonel King wrote a confidential memorandum to the head of the CIA which affirmed that in Cuba there existed a "far-left dictatorship, which if allowed to remain will encourage similar actions against U.S. holdings in other Latin American countries."[15]

King recommended various actions to solve the Cuban problem, one of which was to consider the elimination of Fidel Castro. He affirmed that none of the other Cuban leaders "have the same mesmeric appeal to the masses. Many informed people believe that the disappearance of Fidel would greatly accelerate the fall of the present government."[16]

CIA Director Allen Dulles passed on King's memorandum to the National Security Council a few days later, and it approved the suggestion to form a working group in the Agency which, within a short period of time, could come up with "alternative solutions to the Cuban problem." Thus "Operation 40" was born, taking its name from that of the Special Group formed by the National Security Council to follow the Cuban case which was presided over by Richard Nixon and included Admiral Arleigh Burke, Livingston Merchant of the State Department, National Security Adviser Gordon Gray, and Allen Dulles of the CIA.[17]

Tracy Barnes functioned as head of the Cuban Task Force. He called a meeting on January 18, 1960, in his office in Quarters Eyes, near the Lincoln Memorial in Washington, which the Navy had lent while new buildings were being constructed in Langley. Those who gathered there included the eccentric Howard Hunt, future head of the Watergate team and a writer of crime novels; the egocentric Frank Bender, a friend of Trujillo; Jack Esterline,

---

[14] Report from the G-2 Information Department of the Rebel Army on the activities of the U.S. embassy in Havana. January 1960.

[15] *Alleged assassination plots*, 92.

[16] *Alleged assassination plots*, 93, 94.

[17] Hinckle and Turner, *Deadly secrets*, 42.

who had come straight from Venezuela where he directed a CIA group; psychological warfare expert David A. Phillips and others.[18]

The team responsible for the plans to overthrow the government of Jacobo Arbenz in Guatemala in 1954 was reconstituted, and in the minds of all its members this would be a rerun of the same plan. Barnes talked at length of the goals to be achieved. He explained that Vice-President Richard Nixon was the Cuban "case officer" who had assembled an important group of businessmen headed by George Bush and Jack Crichton, both Texas oilmen, to gather the necessary funds for the operation. Nixon was a protégé of Bush's father Preston who in 1946 had supported Nixon's bid for Congress. In fact, Preston Bush was the campaign strategist that brought Eisenhower and Nixon to the presidency of the United States. With such patrons, Barnes was certain that failure was impossible.

They set to work immediately. They had to come up with a plan to destabilize the Cuban government and extinguish the expectations of social justice which had been ignited in the hemisphere. They created several teams with specific goals and concrete short- and medium-term plans. They assumed that the Cuban revolution could not resist a combined assault of psychological warfare, diplomatic and economic pressures and clandestine activity, all of this backed up by a political structure made up of men in exile who, when the time came, would declare themselves a rebel government which the United States and its allies could publicly recognize and assist.

However, there were several problems. The main one, was the deeply rooted support for Fidel Castro among the Cuban population. Therefore, from the very beginning the physical elimination of the Cuban leader was considered one of the CIA's highest priorities.

There was also the fact that Cuba, being an island, had no borders from which invasions could be organized and directed. The task force analyzed this problem in detail, and finally

---

[18] *Alleged assassination plots*, 93-94.

proposed a strategy of general uprising which consisted in stirring up the whole Cuban population, in order to legitimize a military intervention. Two key elements in the plan were the organization of a "responsible opposition in exile" and the infiltration of several dozen agents into the island, properly trained to deliver the mortal blow.

These specialists viewed the problem as something relatively easy and straight forward. They were convinced that Trujillo's conspiracy and Huber Matos' plot had both failed because of human error in planning the actions. This time things would turn out differently, since the U.S. empire itself was in charge of the operation.

One of Howard Hunt's first jobs when he arrived in Miami was to find an efficient assistant. His mission was to convince "prominent" Cubans there to form a front to back up the operational plans of the CIA in the months ahead.[19] He selected Bernard Baker, the CIA agent who, months earlier, had helped Manuel Artime flee from Cuba. He also talked with Batista supporters, organized into the Anticommunist Crusade. They were a powerful force that could not be ignored. Besides, Colonel King had instructed Hunt to give preferential attention to this group, which was favorably disposed to the United States, and with whom they could do business once their cause triumphed.

Hunt had risen as far as he could in the CIA and knew that he would never be made division chief; therefore this mission suited him perfectly. He would do his job for the Agency while preparing himself for the new life he envisioned as a businessman after the fall of the "Castro regime."

Meanwhile, other plans were underway in Langley. Tracy Barnes and Frank Bender knew that Batista and his supporters had lost all prestige in Cuba and Latin America in general. The Agency was also looking for its own candidates. Two men were particularly favored because they represented two different generations of Cuban politicians: one was Tony Varona, and the

---

[19] Howard Hunt, *Give us this day*, (New York: Popular Library, 1973), 22, 23.

other Manuel Artime Buesa. Another important candidate was the deserter Pedro Luis Díaz Lanz.

Personal interests interfered with the work of the CIA operatives. Finally a deal was struck: the political front would be represented by all of the tendencies in exile, including the Batista supporters. Howard Hunt heaved a sigh of relief; however, he still continued to question the decision by Barnes and Bender not to give that group the preferential treatment that Colonel King, the division chief, had ordered.

On March 4, 1960, *La Coubre*, a ship flying a Belgian flag, exploded in Havana Bay. It was loaded with arms and ammunition destined for the defense of the revolution. The act was a CIA operation carried out by various saboteurs who boarded the ship in its port of origin and placed explosives which were detonated by a device which responded to the change in pressure when the cargo was being unloaded. Seventy-five persons were killed and more than 200 injured as a result. The entire Cuban population turned out at funeral services to honor those fallen in a war that had already begun, although never declared.

The next day, the CIA's Richard Bissell met with members of his Cuban task force. Among those in his office were Colonel King and Inspector Kirkpatrick. Each had a document in front of him marked "top secret," which outlined the basic policies of the Cuba Project:

a. The creation of a responsible and unified Cuban opposition to the Castro regime located outside of Cuba.

b. The development of means for mass communication to the Cuban people as a part of a powerful propaganda offensive.

c. The creation and development of a covert intelligence and action organization within Cuba which would be responsive to the orders and directions of the exile opposition.

d. The development of a paramilitary force outside of Cuba for future guerrilla action. [20]

Finally, the group discussed the justification to be presented to the mass media when reporting on the aggression that was being planned. David Phillips came up with the idea that they would say that the revolution had been "betrayed."

On March 17, 1960, U.S. President Dwight D. Eisenhower signed a National Security Council directive approving "A Program of Covert Action Against the Castro Regime," code named Operation 40.[21] From that moment on, the White House gave the green light to its armies of mercenaries, political schemers, plunderers and assassins for hire to topple the Cuban revolution.

Operation 40 got off the ground rapidly. Hunt's first steps were to form a political infrastructure that would obscure the hand of the U.S. government. It was necessary to form a "responsible opposition" in Florida. That was no easy task. It meant placating all the old political sharks of Cuban politics who were waiting to return to the island. The Batista group wanted the biggest share, having the most significant representation in exile. They also had military cadres and a structure in the principal cities of the United States. On the other hand, there were the followers of Prío and company, and finally the new exiles who demanded their share of the power.

There were differences within the CIA itself. Howard Hunt was a subordinate of Frank Bender in the political front organization, but both represented different tendencies.[22] While one offered his favors to the Batista faction, the other, more pragmatic, felt they should choose figures who were not associated with the old dictatorship. Hunt's protégé, who had been selected by Colonel King, was Dr. Antonio Rubio Padilla, minister of government under Carlos Prío in the 1940s, founder

---

[20] Maxwell Taylor, *Memorandum No. 1*, Narrative of the Anti-Castro Cuban Operation Zapata, June 13, 1961.

[21] Taylor, *Memorandum*.

[22] Hunt, *Give us this day*, 49-50.

of the Radical Liberal Party together with José Ignacio Rasco, and backed by the powerful Cuban bishops. He was friendly with many U.S. businessmen, among them Ambassador William Pawley.

Bender openly opposed Dr. Rubio's candidacy, who he knew had been a faithful collaborator of Batista, and therefore it would be very easy to expose him and bring down the fledgling political front like a house of cards. He appealed to Tracy Barnes, who supported his position, and they struck a compromise: the political wing of the front would be presided over by someone from the Cuban political forum, and the military wing would be led by someone from Batista's army.

Therefore, after much discussion, the "prominent" politician Manuel Antonio ("Tony") de Varona Loredo was selected. He was a man with many influential friends among U.S. businessmen and mafiosos interested in Cuba. Varona had fled to Florida after the Batista coup in 1952 and taken refuge there. He was a prosperous businessman and toward the end of the decade of the 1940s had invested in a real estate company in southern Florida in collusion with the Mafia. Working in the shadow of his friends at the U.S. State Department, he donated a little bit of money, sent a few revolutionaries off on doomed missions, and became a loud-mouthed warrior against the Batista dictatorship from the comfort of his refuge in Florida.

The other person chosen was Colonel Eduardo Martín Elena, who obtained his stripes in the offices of the Columbia Military Base in Havana, the old headquarters of Batista's army. His responsibility would be to select and train the future mercenaries who would be infiltrated into Cuba to "liberate" it from communism.

But there was more. Howard Hunt had another card up his sleeve: Manuel Artime Buesa, the Cuban "hero" of the clandestine struggle who had already earned himself a reputation as a man of action. He had his own plans and could count on the support of the major lay organizations in Cuba. He thought that he could structure the counterrevolutionary movement in such a way that he could draw the attention of the CIA. That way, when the counterrevolution triumphed, he would have control of the internal front and his leadership would be undisputed.

The task of convincing Manuel Artime was arduous. Howard Hunt went through his entire repertoire of arguments to persuade him to join the political exile group. He finally conceded to Artime the possibility of forming his own group inside and outside of Cuba, with logistical and financial support from the CIA.

April 1960 saw the formation of the International Anticommunist Brigade, a phantom organization directed by CIA agent Frank Sturgis for the purpose of preparing a secret network of safe houses, naval installations, boats, planes, warehouses; in short, everything necessary to provide the recruits with a secure base from which to carry out their covert activities. The Brigade would also be responsible for conscripting exiles, administering the training camps and coordinating supply missions for counterrevolutionary groups inside Cuba.

On May 17, 1960, Radio Swan began broadcasting. This radio station sought to influence Cuban public opinion by grossly manipulating information on political events which occurred on the island. This marked the beginning of the airwave aggression that has not only been maintained, but also expanded throughout these many years.[23] The transmitters, with 50 kilowatts of power, were installed on Swan Island in the Atlantic Ocean, off the Honduran coast. They broadcast 24 hours a day in hope of directing clandestine activity and, later, preparing a guerrilla campaign of psychological warfare which would lay the groundwork for an invasion. In the international registries, the station appeared as an affiliate of the Gibraltar Steamship Company. Its mastermind was the spy David A. Phillips.

---

[23] In September 1962, Donald M. Wilson of the United States Information Agency in Washington sent a memorandum to General Edward G. Lansdale regarding short wave, medium wave, FM and television broadcasts to Cuba. Since then, thousands of hours have been beamed at Cuba, including a TV station which is not seen in Cuba. Declassified document.

The first recruits that were to be trained in the arts of subversion, sabotage and assassination arrived in June 1960 on the tiny island of Useppa in the Florida Keys. There were 25 men in the initial group, almost all of them ex-officials of Batista's army, including José Pérez San Román, future military chief of the mercenaries at the Bay of Pigs; Miguel Orozco Crespo, who would become a commander in the Special Missions Group; Jorge Rojas Castellanos, ex-official of the old army and Batista's nephew; Manuel Blanco Navarro, a former *casquito;* and others, most of whom were later captured by Cuban security forces as they disembarked on the coast.

In Guatemala, the CIA station chief, Robert Kendall Davis, asked the local dictator, Miguel Ydigoras Fuentes, for authorization to locate training camps for the mercenary Cubans in his country. That way they would be able to maintain the secrecy necessary to effect the invasion against Cuba. It would also eliminate public evidence that the action originated in the United States.

The Guatemalan government owed a debt to the CIA, and the latter was calling in its chip. The land chosen was the Retalhuleu Farm, renamed Base Trax. Situated in the Pacific zone of the country, it was the property of Roberto Alejos, brother of the Guatemalan ambassador to Washington. It easily lent itself to the construction of an airport and other necessary facilities.

Sometime between June and July 1960, the recruitment offices began functioning in Florida and other states of the union where large numbers of Cubans resided. The plan was to enlist 300 men from which to extract the groups of agents that would infiltrate Cuba and overthrow the government. The head instructor was a Philippine Army Colonel named Napoleón Valeriano, a specialist in anti-guerrilla warfare and known assassin of patriots in his own country.

The initial ideas were extremely pragmatic. According to CIA analysts, the Cuban revolution was forged by a select group whom the people followed blindly. They didn't consider the justice of the cause Fidel's army represented, because for them the people had no will of their own, who followed leaders whether or not they shared their aspirations. Therefore the counter-revolutionary plan consisted of forming groups or teams of five men each, specialists in various subversive methods, who would infiltrate the island to take control of the clandestine movement and lead it to rebellion. Each plan would have its quota of teams, according to the capacity of the counterrevolutionaries and the particular conditions. Pinar del Río, Matanzas, Las Villas and Oriente would be the centers of the guerrilla movement; and in Havana and Camagüey the focus of the struggle would be in the cities.

Each group would have a leader and four men specializing in communications, clandestine operations, psychological warfare, and explosives. In espionage jargon, these groups would be known as infiltration teams. Colonel Valeriano's task was a difficult one, since in spite of the bottomless quarry of potential recruits, he was only able to prepare 85 men, of whom only 35 could be infiltrated in the following months. Nevertheless, of these, 20 were captured. It was no record, but it was certainly a magnificent average for the Cuban G-2 officials.

On June 16, 1960, the U.S. ambassador in Cuba, Philip Bonsal, received an urgent summons from the Cuban Minister of Foreign Relations. He was informed that two of his diplomats had been captured that afternoon by security forces at a meeting with Cuban counterrevolutionaries, and that consequently they had been declared persona non grata and given a few hours within which to leave the island. The attachés Edward L. Sweet and William G. Friedman had been surprised inside a residence at 42nd Street and Fifth Avenue in Miramar where they were instructing various heads of groups in subversive activities. A search of Friedman's house revealed Nazi flags and literature, and he admitted to being a fervent sympathizer of the fascist cause.

The following day, a spokesman for the U.S. State Department, Joseph Reap, accused the Cuban authorities of mistreating his diplomats, since they were not allowed to immediately contact their embassy. Nevertheless, he said nothing about the accusations of the Cuban government concerning the activities in which the two men were involved.

On June 5, in Costa Rica, Manuel Artime announced the founding of his counterrevolutionary organization, the Movement for the Recovery of the Revolution (MRR), declaring that it was the strongest organization in Cuba. Several days later, on June 22, the men who had been selected by the CIA met in Mexico to form the "responsible opposition" which would unite the exile forces. Previously each of them had — like Artime — founded their own counterrevolutionary group, such as Rescate (Rescue), Montecristi, Triple A, and the Christian Democratic Movement.

Those chosen, in addition to Artime, were Tony Varona, Aureliano Sánchez Arango, Justo Carrillo, and José Ignacio Rasco, all with important sponsors in the United States. The object of the so-called Democratic Revolutionary Front (FRD) was to take responsibility for the war, first covert and then overt, which the United States was about to declare against Cuba — giving it a legal cover. However, this coalition was very fragile, and soon, in spite of the efforts of the CIA, it would sink in a sea of ambitions and internal squabbles.

In early July, Richard Bissell called a top secret meeting of his anti-Cuba task force. He wanted them to hear the report of Joseph Scheider, head of the Agency's laboratories and known as the Lucrezia Borgia of the CIA. The scientists had just discovered a new substance derived from LSD which provoked a hallucinatory state in a subject, followed by unconsciousness. The plan consisted of slipping the substance to Fidel Castro during one of his regular TV broadcasts. Then, through a skillful manipulation of the press, it could be declared that the Cuban leader had suffered a bout of temporary insanity, thus undermining his charismatic appeal. However, the operatives failed to find anyone who could carry out the plan.

From the beginning the assassination of Fidel Castro and other Cuban leaders was another of the secret plans with the highest priority within Operation 40. A team of professional hit men was contracted by the CIA for these jobs, and dozens of assassination plots were planned against Fidel Castro, Raúl

Castro, Che Guevara, Juan Almeida Bosque, Carlos Rafael Rodríguez and others.

On July 22, the CIA station in Havana telegraphed a message of the utmost urgency to Langley, which reported that one of their agents had penetrated Raúl Castro's bodyguards and offered his services to arrange an "accident." A few hours later Jim Noel received approval for the plan. The case officer in charge of the operation rushed from the embassy to the prearranged meeting to instruct the would-be assassin. At this precise moment — when nothing could be done because the orders had already been given — a second cable arrived at the embassy, deauthorizing the action. As always, plausible denial was in operation. If anything went wrong, they could allege that the plans had not been approved by the higher authorities at the CIA. [24]

In July, on the initiative of Allen Dulles, a secret meeting was held with the four leaders of the Democratic Revolutionary Front (FRD) and the Democratic presidential candidate, John F. Kennedy. The purpose was to inform the politician of the plans that were underway to bring down the Cuban revolution and to introduce him to the future leaders of the neighboring country.

In August 1960, the CIA laboratory came up with a new product: thallium salts which had a depilatory effect. The CIA then waited for an opportunity to get near Fidel to use this powder to make him lose his beard, which they considered to be the key to his charisma. Another invention placed at the disposal of the CIA arsenal was a chemical agent that could be applied to tobacco. If Fidel were to smoke it he would suffer a sudden disorientation which could be used to launch a press campaign accusing him of dementia, and thus undermining his authority and prestige. However, the Agency's operatives lacked the elements in Cuba which would enable them to carry out these plans and so they remained shelved for some time, to the understandable frustration of their inventors.

In August, the plans for Operation 40 abruptly changed course. Reports arriving from Cuba were alarming, since they

---

[24] *Alleged assassination plots*, 92-94.

revealed that the government enjoyed a high level of popular support. Therefore it was decided to place the emphasis on organizing an armed expedition which, with or without internal support, would be capable of sweeping Fidel Castro off the island. Some $13 million was earmarked for the formation of a mercenary brigade of approximately 600 men. They were confident that landing a fully-equipped and well-armed troop backed by the United States would cause the government to fall within a few days, as it had in Guatemala in 1954.

Recruitment in Florida and other states was stepped up and new instructors were added at the training camps in Guatemala. Counterrevolutionary emissaries were sent to Cuba to reinforce the internal front and assure support for the armed actions that were being planned. Various clandestine cells of counter-revolutionary organizations, trained and armed by the CIA, operated on the island. One of their chiefs, Rogelio González Corso, alias Francisco, had been infiltrated not long before to unify the opposition groups under the banner of the FRD. These would form the base which would work with the infiltration teams being prepared in Guatemala and Panama.

With the rise of these activities, hundreds of new Cuban organizations were created. Many of them succumbed without ever firing a shot, destroyed by the internal power struggles over the favor of the CIA. Others caused serious damage to the economy and took the lives of Cuban citizens. Among the most important of these groups, in addition to the Democratic Revolutionary Front were the Martí Democratic Movement (MDM), the People's Revolutionary Movement (MRP), Rescate, the Second National Front of the Escambray, the National Liberation Army (ELN), the Armed Forces of Liberation (FAL) and many more.

Simultaneously, CIA agents in the U.S. embassy continued their search for new opportunities for action. During the second half of 1960 it came to their attention that the revolutionary government was establishing relations with the Soviet Union and the People's Republic of China. They immediately organized plans to find out what buildings would be used for the offices of these diplomatic representations. The first technical operation launched was against the Soviet headquarters. According to their informant, it would be located on the top floor of the Rosita de Horneado Apartments, today the Hotel Sierra Maestra, in the Miramar neighborhood. Several months earlier they had recruited the son of the owner of that building, Alfredo Izaguirre de la Riva, a journalist with profound anticommunist convictions.

CIA headquarters sent a technician named Mel Beck who, with Izaguirre's help, installed two microphones in the luxurious living room of the penthouse. The system would automatically go into action when the room lights were turned on. The control post, located in a neighbor's apartment, would record all the conversations that took place there. The job was perfect, except for one thing: the Soviets never used that apartment.

The second technical penetration was against the Chinese news agency Xinhua, located in the Retiro Médico building at the corner of 23rd Avenue and N Street in Vedado. Agent Mario Nordio, a U.S. citizen, was sent to rent the apartment above the one to be used by the news service. When everything was ready the CIA dispatched three technicians — Eustace D. Brunet, Edmundo R. Taranski and Daniel L. Carswell — to drill holes in the floor and place the microphones. The specialists set to work. They operated out of a safe house in the same building, the apartment of Marjorie Lennox, a secretary at the embassy, who supplied them with food and drinks while they worked. Everything went fine until September 8, when G-2 agents captured them by surprise. Nordio fled and sought refuge in the home of another spy-diplomat Robert L. Need, but it did him little good. The next day, after a public denunciation, they were all expelled from the country.

This exposé did not stop the activities, however. In Washington, Bissell met with Colonels J.C. King and Sheffield Edwards, the CIA's Director of the Office of Security. The main topic was the need to eliminate Fidel Castro.[25] Edwards proposed a new alternative, giving the job to the U.S. organized gambling

---

[25] *Alleged assassination plots*, 74-76.

syndicate, who had seen its casinos expropriated and had been expelled from Cuba. The plan would be carried out through an old operative, Jim O'Connell, who would use one of his agents, Robert Maheu, to contact elements in the Mafia.

Maheu was an ex-FBI agent who had begun his career in 1954 as a private investigator. He had earned a reputation in the Agency for carrying out risky operations, and had prevented more than one CIA employee from being caught with his hands in the cookie jar. The mafioso chosen by Maheu was John Rosselli, an underworld character connected to Las Vegas gambling whom he had known since the mid-1950s when he had cultivated the image of a tough guy.

On September 9, Rosselli and Maheu met in the Brown Derby Restaurant in Beverly Hills.[26] There the agent told the mafioso that some high government officials needed Fidel Castro out of the way, and asked him to recruit someone who could do the job. Rosselli hesitated, but finally said he would do it for the government. He accepted the assignment on the condition that he meet with an official representative. Four days later, in the Hotel Plaza in New York, he was given the guarantees he required.

Fidel Castro was about to visit New York in order to take part in the UN General Assembly, where he wanted to explain what was really going on in Cuba and answer the systematic defamation campaign by the international media.

This was the occasion that the CIA operatives who had been following his movements were waiting for. A room in the Waldorf Astoria Hotel had been rented for the police escorts placed at the disposal of the heads of state. The plan consisted of recruiting the head of this group of bodyguards to surreptitiously place a box of cigars in the Cuban leader's hotel room. These cigars would contain a small explosive charge, designed to blow his head off. The policeman refused angrily, affirming that his mission was to protect Castro, not kill him.

Fidel returned to Cuba and the CIA-Mafia plans continued on their course. Rosselli and Maheu moved to Miami and in mid-

---

[26] *Alleged assassination plots*, 75.

October of that year, the mafioso introduced his accomplice to two individuals he trusted completely: Salvatore Giancana and Santos Trafficante, who would be those charged with finding executioners among the Cuban exiles.

The Mafia's original idea was to recruit one of Fidel's bodyguards to carry out the crime. They thought about a gangland-style slaying, where the victim would be simply gunned down. However, the idea was soon abandoned as dangerous and impractical when the proper person couldn't be found to carry it out. At the end of November, Giancana met with O'Connell and proposed another form of assassination where the perpetrator would have a better chance to escape with his life. They both thought poison was the preferred method.[27] Joseph Scheider was called in again, and his laboratories set to work.

Meanwhile, in Cuba the destabilization plans continued at an accelerated pace. Sturgis' group had prepared a guerrilla band to infiltrate the eastern part of the country and ignite the flames of rebellion. On October 5, a detachment of mercenaries made up of 27 of Batista's henchmen and at least two North Americans disembarked in Navas Bay, between the towns of Moa and Baracoa. The head of the group was the well-known criminal Armentino Feria, alias *El Indio* (the Indian), who had been a captain in one of Batista's paramilitary gangs. Within a few days they were all captured by the Rebel Army and peasant militia, who had followed them from the moment of their arrival. Among those arrested was the Yankee Tony Salvat, Feria's military adviser. Their adventure ended in a resounding defeat.

On October 8, Rebel Army forces completed an important operation in the Escambray mountain stronghold. The counter-revolutionaries, encouraged by the CIA, had formed armed detachments there which committed crimes and abuses against the peasant population. The enemy objective consisted of preparing a military force in the rear of the revolutionary troops so that at the proper time, when the mercenary brigade landed on the Cuban coasts, the supply lines and rear guard could be

---

[27] *Alleged assassination plots*, 80.

annihilated. Their other mission was to create an atmosphere of chaos and destabilization which would look like a civil war and could justify U.S. intervention.

Counterrevolutionary leaders Porfirio Ramírez, Plinio Prieto and Sinesio Walsh reported to Tony Varona's FRD through his brother-in-law José Ruiz Sánchez, alias Comandante Augusto, who coordinated with the U.S. embassy the supply of arms, ammunition and logistical support sent by the CIA. In September, as part of this backup, they parachuted in a U.S. adviser named Richard Pecoraro who met with the various bandit chiefs to see what they needed and recommend organizational measures to improve the combat readiness of the troops on the eve of the Bay of Pigs invasion.

In the Escambray operation, known in Cuba as the "Struggle Against the Bandits," the popular militias played a key role, destroying the main counterrevolutionary groups and seizing countless military weapons and supplies.

Meanwhile, in the Cuban cities the all-out struggle continued between these groups and the security forces who, with the help of the people, were dismantling them. One important case became public in the month of October, concerning the "Opera" operation, in which the G-2 penetrated the CIA station in the U.S. embassy, headed by Colonel Erickson S. Nichols and Major Robert Van Horn, both military attachés. The objective of these spies was to organize the counterrevolution in the city of Havana. They were to carry out a broad subversive plan which included blowing up the Ñico López Oil Refinery and the Tallapiedra Electrical Plant, promoting uprisings in the Escambray and carrying out attempts on the lives of leaders of the revolution, Fidel Castro in particular.

Among the most important CIA agents involved in these plans was Geraldine Shapman, a Bostonian married to a millionaire tobacco manufacturer. She was recruited by Major Van Horn and was one of the key persons coordinating the arms shipments to the Escambray. She was arrested on November 15, when a large cache of weapons and explosives was found in an apartment she owned in the elegant Biltmore neighborhood — now called Siboney — in the municipality of Marianao.[28]

In her statements to the Cuban authorities, Shapman explained the preparations to invade Cuba that were underway in Florida and Guatemala. She herself had rented a house in Miami which served as a way station for recruits en route to the camps in Central America. Cuba once again denounced these activities, but few wished to listen, for the anti-Cuba campaign being carried out had bought off presidents and silenced the mass media throughout the entire continent.

On December 1, 1960, Richard Bissell called an urgent meeting of his anti-Cuba group of operatives. Hours earlier they had received a cable from Robert Kendall Davis, CIA station chief in Guatemala. The message read:

> Urgent: Bissell, Kirkpatrick, and Barnes:
> The brigade has suffered a profound demoralization. Pepe San Román refuses to continue in command of the troops due to Varona's spadework to make one of his own men military chief. It is necessary to end the political discussions and pacify the members of the expedition. Nobody is showing up for training and there is widespread insubordination. Awaiting instructions. Stop.[29]

The men in Bissell's office looked at each other in silence. Then each one expressed his point of view. It was clear that if they didn't take measures in time, all the effort and money invested would be lost and, even worse, the government of Fidel Castro would be strengthened. The conclusion was clear. They would clip Varona's wings and the CIA would make San Román head of the operation. There was no time for a political disquisition.

---

[28] *30 años. Historia de la Seguridad Cubana.* Historical Commission of Cuban State Security. Central Political Directorate, Ministry of the Interior, 1989. La Opera Case.

[29] Report from the Intelligence Information Department of the Revolutionary Armed Forces (DIIFAR) on Cuban counterrevolutionary activities in Guatemala. January 1961.

The deputy director for analysis spoke up. He was worried about the constant reports of the support enjoyed by Fidel Castro among broad sectors of the Cuban population. If that were so, the 600 men being prepared would amount to nothing. It would be necessary to increase the number of troops and arm them with better weapons from the U.S. military arsenal. They all agreed. A few days later the Special Group of the National Security Council approved a budget increase and ordered the Pentagon to supply all the arms and specialists required for the operation against Cuba, which then received the code name "Pluto."

In November, the mercenaries training at Base Trax underwent a baptism of fire. In Puerto Barrios there was a rebellion of young Guatemalan soldiers who sought to liberate their country from its military dictatorship. It was time for the trainees to show what they had learned. A detachment of 200 was sent to this port city to collaborate with government troops in quashing the rebellion.

Trax by then had become a complex military installation with an air base and a mountain camp which the mercenaries nicknamed "Garrapatenango," a play on the work "tick," the insect that plagued them night and day. On the Atlantic coast of Nicaragua, a few hours away by plane, they had established a naval base from which to launch the invasion.

Air and sea traffic back and forth between Costa Rica, Nicaragua, Guatemala and Florida was intense. Ships and planes carrying men and merchandise constantly traveled the routes and shrewd Cubans, North Americans and other advocates of free enterprise began the prosperous business of trading in contraband military weapons and supplies for "the cause of liberty." Later, inspired by the success of this enterprise, whiskey became the principal commodity, to be supplanted later by blood and finally, drugs.

The pioneer drug runners in America were the CIA and their associates.[30] Their planes and ships transported thousands of tons of cocaine, heroin, marijuana and other narcotics. When the

---

[30] Hinckle and Turner, *Deadly secrets*, XXXVIII.

entire story of this aggression and bloodshed is finally written; when all the information is declassified and made available to the public, then the macabre details of the plans the CIA used to try to topple the Cuban government will be revealed, along with the true facts about how in this process officials and agents of the U.S. Central Intelligence Agency enriched themselves.

CHAPTER 5

Operation Pluto

On November 4, 1960, John F. Kennedy was elected the 35th president of the United States, after defeating the ultra-conservative Richard Nixon by a narrow margin.

One of the heated topics of the electoral campaign was the Cuban "problem." Since the middle of the year, Kennedy, as a candidate for the presidency, had been informed about the invasion plans being prepared by the Eisenhower administration. Nevertheless he acted as if he were ignorant of them. In his pre-election speeches, taking advantage of the fact that his opponent, given his position, could say nothing about the plans, he criticized the incumbent administration for its apparent inertia in the face of events on the neighboring island. Years later, in his memoirs, Nixon bitterly lamented this underhanded trick since, if the truth be told, if the Bay of Pigs had a progenitor, it was Nixon.

Nixon's press secretary of that era, Herbert Klein, would later write:

> From the start of the 1960 campaign, many of us were convinced that Cuba could be the deciding issue in a close election. Certainly, in retrospect, it was one of the decisive factors in what was the closest presidential election of modern history. . . .
>
> Only four of us on the Nixon staff shared the secret that the refugees were being trained for an eventual assault on

Castro and a return to Cuba. We had stern instructions not to talk about this . . . . [31]

On September 23, 1960, Kennedy proposed in a campaign speech that "the forces fighting for freedom in exile and in the mountains of Cuba should be sustained and assisted."[32] A few days later, on October 6, he urged "encouraging those liberty-loving Cubans who are leading the resistance to Castro."[33] He alluded to the "Communist menace that has been permitted to arise under our very noses, only 90 miles from our shores,"[34] and concluded by accusing the government of irresponsibility for its supposed ineffectual policy against the tiny island.

In spite of this, some prominent figures of the Kennedy administration insist to this day that he really had no advance information about the planned invasion and that his declarations were legitimate political attacks.

On November 18, Allen Dulles and Richard Bissell, two top CIA officials, called on Kennedy at his vacation home in Palm Beach and gave him the details of the anti-Cuba operation. In several hours of conversation, the President-elect was given a broad outline of the program, which was already quite advanced. By that time, the CIA had arrived at the decision to build up an assault brigade which would land in Cuba, then capture a beachhead, install a provisional government and ask for help from the "democratic" countries of the continent — that is, the United States, who would generously send its Marines to liberate the "suffering Cubans" from communism.

When President Kennedy's advisers learned of the details of the Cuban project, they were upset. Cuba was a bad example for the hemisphere, and the United States shouldn't permit communism to take hold at its very doorstep; but they were all too familiar with the CIA operatives and the shamelessness with which they normally acted.

---

[31] Hinckle and Turner, *Deadly secrets*, 37.

[32] Nixon, *Six crises*, 353.

[33] Kennedy, *The speeches of*, 515.

[34] Kennedy, *The speeches of*, 510-511.

Operation Pluto[35] was really nothing more than Trujillo's old plan: a mercenary brigade landing on the beaches near the city of Trinidad in the southern part of Las Villas Province, storming the city and then, with the support of the guerrillas in the Escambray mountains, cutting communications and installing the provisional government where it could call for the help that was waiting.

All that seemed too brazen to hide the involvement of the U.S. government, and this did not fit in with the plans of the group of presidential advisers who argued that Latin America should become one of the nation's new priorities. A volcano was building up there and once it began erupting there would be no way to stop it. The continent demanded a new perspective, and for that it would be necessary to erase the image of the "Big Stick Diplomacy" which characterized previous U.S. administrations. This was the main reason they cautioned the President to be prudent. They needed to be more subtle in approaching the problem and assaulting the city of Trinidad was no way to do it.

Kennedy spent the end of 1960 considering this and other urgent matters: the question of West Berlin, the situation in Indochina, and an endless number of foreign policy problems where the United States had to take a position.

On December 16, 1960, G-2 headquarters assessed the counterrevolutionary activity in the capital during the last few months of the year. Among the observations, it was pointed out:

> Between the months of September and December of the present year, more than 50 violations of air space have occurred in the Province of Havana, many of them for the purpose of distributing counterrevolutionary propaganda and dropping bombs on strategic objectives in the capital.
>
> On September 16, unknown persons fired at a national militia vehicle, and wounded several of its occupants. The 28th of that month, three bombs exploded during a mass rally near the Presidential Palace; and a fourth, in Revolution

---

[35] *30 años*, Operation Pluto.

Square. Thirty-four incidents of sabotage and terrorist acts against the population were reported during this same period.

On October 5, a subject was detained while trying to place a bomb on G Street and 15th. On the 7th, a strong explosion occurred in the Firestone Tire Factory after an unknown plane flew over it. On the 16th and 17th, several vehicles occupied by unknown persons shot at two Agrarian Reform Institute automobiles, wounding the drivers and all of the passengers. In addition, 35 incidents of sabotage and terrorist acts against the population were reported.

On November 23, several combat planes with no markings flew over the San Antonio de los Baños Air Base. That month, 80 incidents of sabotage and terrorist acts took place.

In December, an unidentified aircraft dropped counter-revolutionary proclamations over the Las Cabañas Military Fortress and 57 incidents of sabotage and terrorist acts were reported in the capital. Among the most significant was a bomb planted in the University of Havana which, in addition to causing damage, seriously injured a student.

In December, terrorist activities increased throughout the country, including arson in a number of tobacco houses in Pinar del Río; 29 terrorist acts in Las Villas, including the murder of several peasants by the bandits; 16 acts of sabotage and an assault on a police station in Camagüey; and seven major acts of sabotage in Santiago de Cuba.[36]

The Puerto Barrios adventure enhanced the prestige of the mercenaries who participated in it. The instructors from the United States and other countries praised them and held them up as an example for the inexperienced troops.

Among the most seasoned of the soldiers were Félix Rodríguez, Segundo Borges, José Basulto, Javier Souto, Edgar

---

[36] Report from the Information Department of Cuban State Security. December 16, 1960.

Sopo and Rafael García Rubio. They didn't know that the experience they acquired had earned them the green light to form the infiltration teams that months later would penetrate Cuba to set in march an operation whose slogan, "Silent War and Strategy of Terror," meant destabilizing the country and creating propitious conditions for the military aggression.

Colonel Napoleón Valeriano was pleased with his pupils. They had learned quickly the techniques of destruction and death. He didn't know that the CIA had changed its plans and soon he and the other instructors would be unemployed when Army Colonel Jack Hawkins and his colleagues, the Green Berets, would take charge of the brigade to turn it into a real military unit.

The name of the brigade, "2506," came from the dog tag number of one of the first recruits, who was killed during a training accident. The brains at the CIA thought that this number might confuse the Cuban agents, but the latter — whose numbers were smaller than imagined, but whose dedication and valor was incalculable — used their prowess to insure that the Cuban authorities could not be tricked.

William "Rip" Robertson and Grayston Lynch were among the trainers who became de facto adjunct chiefs during the invasion. Both had helped the counterrevolutionary cause from the beginning, when they joined Frank Sturgis in the Anticommunist Brigade, a front organization created for the Cuba invasion. They keep reappearing throughout the entire anti-Cuba saga, and some researchers in the United States and elsewhere have suggested that they participated in the Kennedy assassination.

The most popular of the two was undoubtedly "Rip" Robertson, a huge Texan who was a Navy captain during the Second World War. During the 1954 coup in Guatemala, he ordered the bombing of a presumably Soviet ship, anchored in a port in that Central American country. But he was mistaken and the mercenary plane sank a British vessel, for which the U.S. government paid a one and a half million dollar indemnity. The CIA punished him by cutting him off from their work, and until

1960 nobody wanted to even hear his name. For that reason, Robertson was determined to excel in this assignment in order to redeem himself.

One of his buddies from previous adventures had recently arrived at Retalhuleu. He was the pilot Robert Plumlee, who had worked with Robertson in Florida, sending weapons and propaganda to the counterrevolutionaries in Cuba. The aviators recruited from the Alabama Air National Guard in Birmingham and some instructors from the U.S. Air Force had come down to the base. They were to be given the responsibility of destroying the few planes of the Cuban Air Force and providing backup for the brigade, once it landed. An airstrip had been constructed at Base Trax, practically parallel to a railroad track, and the passengers riding by each day would admire the planes lined up there awaiting orders to attack.

Soon the time had come to choose the launching point for the invasion, and the CIA once again appealed to its old friend Anastasio Somoza, dictator of neighboring Nicaragua. Puerto Cabezas, on that country's Atlantic coast, was the ideal spot. It had a wharf and an airstrip; and furthermore, it was sufficiently out of the way to avoid indiscreet stares. The new base was christened "Tide," and the airport was called "Happy Valley."

Activity was on the increase at Base Trax that month of December 1960. Flights were constantly arriving from Florida, carrying dozens of new recruits, which now included people from all strata of pre-revolutionary Cuban society. The sons of the great capitalist families and landlords gathered there with Batista's *casquitos* and henchmen along with lumpen elements who had fled the island when they discovered that the revolution had declared itself the enemy of vagrancy and idleness.

The installations at the base had been converted into a military camp in the best West Point style. Order and discipline had domesticated the raw recruits, and the Cuban officials, for the most part from the ranks of Batista's army, began forming units and correcting the errors. The exiled leaders visited the camps frequently, not exactly to encourage the "seasoned warriors," but rather to increase their own popularity, since the campaigning had already begun for the political race to set up the new government on the island once the revolution had been smashed.

So Tony Varona was there, along with Manuel Artime, José Ignacio Rasco, Aureliano Sánchez, Justo Carrillo and other well-known sharks to make a show of their support. The troops waited anxiously for these moments, and no one missed the opportunity to shake hands or smile fawningly on their favorite. Political maneuvering was well under way. Many of the conscripts aspired to become political sergeants of the new leaders when the time came to divide the booty of the holy war they were waging.

Nevertheless, this "political" work had a number of drawbacks. There were serious divergences among the different groups that made up the brigade.[37] Tony Varona had imposed former colonel Eduardo Martín Elena as military chief of the FRD, but the CIA and Artime's group didn't accept him. Tempers were heating up, above all, after the appointment of former *casquito* José Pérez San Román as the commander of the brigade. The Agency favored him, since he belonged to the select group of recruits trained on the island of Useppa in the Florida Keys. Moreover, Richard Bissell had insisted that the command of the brigade be in the hands of young soldiers, not obviously linked to the dictatorship, in order to mask his preference for the Batista faction.

Toward the end of December, more conflicts broke out. Varona had taken advantage of the arrival of new mercenaries to send orders to his men. He told them to go on strike at the camp, demanding the replacement of San Román and his group and the reinstatement of Martín Elena.

One morning the U.S. officials were awakened by angry voices rebuking them for showing favoritism to San Román. The situation was getting more complicated, since the mercenaries took their weapons and threatened general insubordination. After several discussions with the leaders, agreement was reached. The

---

[37] Declarations by Humberto Sorí Marín to Cuban State Security. April 1961.

CIA officials would send a cable to Washington explaining their demands, and they would lay down their arms and wait for the response from Uncle Sam.

When the cable arrived at Langley, it produced a tremendous uproar. Just who were those dirty Cubans to rebel, Tracy Barnes wanted to know. Didn't they know that in the same manner that they were sent to combat the insubordinate Guatemalan army forces in Puerto Barrios, the army of this country would be sent to smash them? Finally, prudence prevailed and Frank Bender went to see Tony Varona.

Varona was waiting impatiently to intercede with the mutineers and restore order to the brigade. But, as the old politico would recall years later, "the Americans are unpredictable." They put him on a plane, together with other members of the FRD, and took him directly to Base Trax. There a mean-looking Yankee warned him to pacify the recruits — and confirm San Román's leadership because, if he didn't, he would be chased from there to the Holy Sepulcher.

There is no sacrifice too great for a "selfless patriot," Varona observed as he stepped up to an improvised platform and embraced San Román, soothing the tempers and swearing with misty eyes that he would be involved in no more intrigue. The journalists who accompanied the party took photos, and several days later there was a news report of the visit by FRD leaders to the camps where "seasoned troops were being prepared to liberate the long-suffering Cuba from communism."

On January 1, 1961, the U.S. government decided to unilaterally break diplomatic and consular relations with the Republic of Cuba. The pretext was the usual one: U.S. democracy could not coexist with a communist regime just 90 miles away. Several months earlier the State Department had recalled its ambassador in Havana, Philip Bonsal. The purpose was quite evident: Eisenhower wanted to clear the path for his successor to carry out the aggressive plans without political obstacles or diplomatic complications.

Although the CIA office in Havana knew of the intentions of the President, and for several months had been preparing to withdraw, there were still many contacts to be made which were essential to guarantee that their links were secure. In addition, they had to wait for the agents being trained in Panama to arrive so that they could take over attending to the principal groups. Thus, when the notice of the diplomatic rupture arrived, it caught them off guard.

CIA station chief James Noel met with his closest collaborators and gave them specific orders. "It is necessary to insure at all costs the link with our principal agents," he explained. Those attending this meeting included Colonel Samuel Kail, Eulalia Wall, Major Robert Van Horn, David Morales, Captain Charles Clark, Benjamin Evans and Hugh Kessler. In recent months they had lost some highly qualified personnel to the Cuban G-2, men such as Robert Wichea, William Friedman, Arthur Avignon and the phlegmatic Edwin Sweet, who were essential at a time like this. Everything was supposed to have been left in their hands, but they had been expelled from the country when their activities were uncovered, and now that problem had to be dealt with.

Francisco Muñoz Olivé was an old CIA agent. He had been recruited in the 1950s when he worked as a policeman in Batista's Bureau of Investigations. First he carried out a few minor spy tasks among his coworkers; later, after the CIA had tested his loyalty, he was given more important jobs. The triumph of the revolution surprised him, and he wasn't able to leave the country. Besides, since he had committed no known crimes, he remained for some time in the police force. The local CIA station, valuing the meticulous zeal with which he carried out his missions, assigned him to penetrate the new political institutions being created until, one day in 1959, he was fired because of his shady past.

Then he met David S. Morales, an attaché at the embassy and a CIA official whose nom de guerre was Moraima. Muñoz Olivé met with the official in a home in the Santos Suárez neighborhood, taking advantage of the fact that since Morales was Hispanic, his presence would arouse no suspicion among the people in the neighborhood. The news of the breaking of diplomatic relations took him by surprise. That morning he had received an emergency signal from Morales, and he rushed to the meeting. There he found his officer with several bottles of a chemical for writing secret messages, and after a quick and improvised training session he was given an address in Miami, a few dollars, a theatrical good-bye, and assurances that they would soon meet again. His main task was to gather information about the strength of the Rebel Army. He knew that arms and equipment was arriving from Czechoslovakia, but he didn't know in what quantities. Finding out would be the task of Agent Frank, the pseudonym used by the spy.

They were unable to contact each other within the agreed-upon time frame. Only months later, using a courier disguised as a tourist, was the CIA able to reestablish contact with the agent and put him back in action. Frank was taken prisoner many years later, after an enormous espionage effort, and it wasn't until the late 1970s that he was able to finally meet with Morales, who by that time was retired from the CIA and had become the sheriff of an obscure U.S. county.[38]

In mid-December a group of 84 men arrived at Fort Gulick in the Panama Canal Zone. They had all come from the camps in Guatemala where they had distinguished themselves as the most dedicated recruits. A North American using the pseudonym of Bill met them and quickly explained their new duties, saying they were "going to make up a top secret unit that must guarantee the landing of the brigade in Cuba. There we have many more men ready to fight communism, but they need training and more than that, leadership, command; and this will be your task."

He reviewed the formation and, drawing out each word to arouse more interest, he continued, "We are going to make up two teams composed of specialists in explosives, intelligence, guerrilla struggle and psychological warfare that will act as a group so that when D-Day arrives the communists will be crazy, disorganized and above all will lose their heads when their main

---

[38] Report from Cuban State Security.

command posts are annihilated. We have given these teams the name . . . Grey."

The Yankee gazed attentively at the men lined up in front of him and taking a clipboard which contained a long list of names, began to call them one by one. They included Miguel A. Orozco Crespo, Félix Rodríguez Mendigutía, Manuel Puig Miyar, Manuel Reyes Reyes, Jorge García Rubio, Emilio Rivero Caro and Pedro Cuéllar.

The course began with training in the use of different types of weapons. Then they studied explosives and the booby traps that could be set with them. Later they moved on to guerrilla warfare, clandestine communications, propaganda and psychological warfare, intelligence gathering, and methods of compartmentalization and security. Air and maritime pickup completed the preparation. The training included several hours devoted to the organization of urban and rural groups which were to act on the plans designed by the CIA for 1961.

One of the recurring themes in the course was the compartmentalization which should take place. The drawbacks of large structures were explained, and the fact that smaller cells would be tougher for the Cuban G-2 to penetrate. They were also schooled in interrogation and learned the significance of different degrees of torture. Finally they were ready and their transfer was arranged to safe houses in Florida and New Orleans. There the five-man groups that had been formed were to wait for their infiltration into Cuba which was scheduled to commence in late January 1961.

This and other evidence related here prove that the CIA counted on an internal counterrevolution to help carry out its invasion plan. It is true that in the days prior to April 17 they did not alert their agents. But was it necessary to alert them, after dozens of clandestine infiltrations of arms, explosives and trained men? Was it necessary when everyone knew that the mercenaries had arrived in Puerto Cabezas, Nicaragua, and boarded the boats? Was it necessary when Radio Swan constantly called for an internal rebellion and warned that an invasion by "Cuban patriots" was being prepared somewhere on the continent; when it was loudly gossiped about in Miami *gusano* circles? When the subversives operating in Cuba were searching for secure hideouts to avoid capture, when they were preparing weapons and destroying buildings, warehouses and factories, and murdering workers and members of the militia?

It is obviously false that the failure of the the Bay of Pigs invasion was due to inaction of the internal counterrevolution for lack of a proper signal. They were all on guard, but the U.S. analysts and strategists could not predict the response of the Cuban people, who donned militia uniforms and wiped out the internal fifth column in a few short hours.

The breaking of relations with Cuba by the United States was a kind of signal for those who could not imagine the island free of U.S. tutelage that more direct attacks were on the way to put an end to the revolutionary experiment. Many opted to take refuge in Miami where they could participate in the plans for the invasion or at least, by their presence, earn the right to a share in the spoils once the revolution was destroyed.

Humberto Sorí Marín and Aldo Vera Serafín were among these individuals. Waiting for them there was Alberto Fernández, the wealthy landowner and founder of Revolutionary Unity, the organization with which they had both been conspiring for months. Fernández had owned sugar plantations in Cuba, and when he left the country — afraid that once the peasants learned to read and write they would want a piece of land — he contacted the CIA and became intensely involved in subversive activities. He had purchased a World War II submarine chaser, outfitted it with artillery, christened it *Tejana III* and used it periodically to covertly bring weapons into Cuba and smuggle out counter-revolutionaries who were being pursued.

As soon as Sorí Marín and Aldo Vera arrived in Miami, Fernández introduced them to Howard Hunt so that he could hear first hand the latest news of the Cuban underground and the plans which, according to them, would liquidate the revolution within a few weeks. Hunt was interested and listened to them attentively. He also had personal interests, and hoped to be rewarded for all the effort and sleepless nights that those Cubans had cost him in their fight against communism. Perhaps he thought that if their plan was good enough he could keep the information from Langley, and then at the proper moment exploit it for his own benefit.

Sorí Marín explained their plan for a military rebellion; in other words, a coup d'etat. He said they could count on elements at the military base in San Antonio de los Baños, several Navy ships, and the main police stations in the capital. Before they fled they had met with some of the leaders of the counter-revolutionary Student Directorate who had promised to seize the University of Havana and direct the insurrection from there. Sorí Marín had two guerrilla groups, one in the Sierra de los Organos in Pinar del Río, and the other in the mountains of Mayarí in Oriente Province. They only needed weapons and, above all, explosives, a little money and, should it become necessary, the recognition of the U.S. government.

Moreover, there was a special component of the plan that few knew about: the assassination of Fidel Castro. They had a man who worked in the National Savings and Housing Institute (INAV), a body that Fidel frequently visited to keep himself informed about the state of its projects. In early April, the Cuban Prime Minister was scheduled to attend a meeting to analyze Havana's housing program to provide shelter for the hundreds of families who lived in subhuman conditions, and this would be the ideal time to place a bomb in the meeting hall to consummate the crime.

After the assassination of the Cuban leader, the military and police stations where the plotters had connections would be captured, the university would be occupied, and an extensive wave of sabotage and terrorism would be unleashed which, together with the guerrilla activity, would provide the final blow to bring down the revolution.

Howard Hunt got up from his seat as soon as Sorí Marín finished speaking and he paced up and down the room for a long time. It was too attractive a project not to take advantage of. There were only a few problems, since the government in exile which would declare war on Fidel Castro and take responsibility for the invasion was almost entirely in place. It had taken months of work to get so many political caciques to come to an agreement, and this plan might revive the conflicts and destroy the precarious unity that had been achieved. He needed time to think and work out a solution, therefore he convinced them of the importance of his consulting with a few people. He promised to give them an answer within two days, as long as — and this he emphasized forcefully — no one were to learn of the conversation.

That afternoon Howard Hunt met with his friend Tony Varona. He recognized the abilities of this political shark, and decided to consult with him about the plans, realizing that he would have to be open with him. Varona was in disgrace with the CIA chiefs after the Guatemala affair but he was the best candidate Hunt could find.

After the necessary introduction, Hunt explained the details of the plan proposed by Sorí Marín and Aldo Vera. As he did, his listener's eyes became unusually bright, and when he finished, Varona congratulated him effusively. "I think it's an excellent plan, and I have only a few comments. You know that there are many ambitious men in the FRD, and that you and I should keep this to ourselves. I have an idea: we could name a leadership to unify the counterrevolution in Cuba, as a natural counterpart to the FRD or the council which we must then create. Naturally, these leaders will return to carry out the plans and at the hour of triumph their merits will be greater. The general coordinator will be a man I trust completely and he will be given the help requested; that will be your responsibility. In other words, I'll give him the political endorsement and you give him the resources. . . . What do you think?"

"It sounds reasonable to me," agreed Hunt. "I'm only worried about Artime and his men in Cuba who must know something."

"Fine, my friend," responded Varona. "We can make Artime's man the link in Havana between this group and the CIA and then you'll stay on good terms with him and your superiors will suspect nothing."

"Agreed," smiled Hunt. "And what shall we call this political creature we're creating?"

"The Front for Revolutionary Unity!" responded Varona.[39]

José Joaquín Sanjenís Perdomo was by nature an opportunist. He had been among the first to flee Cuba when they realized that the revolution was going to change the country's socioeconomic structures. His dreams of wealth would never materialize on that path and as soon as he arrived in the United States he enlisted as a CIA agent. He quickly became an informer on his own colleagues when he proposed to his chiefs the creation of an organization to spy on the mercenaries in Guatemala.

What he was really doing was laying the groundwork for the new police force which he assumed would be created after the overthrow of the revolution. He had the backing of his friend David Phillips, who was in charge of the psychological warfare team, whose mission consisted in coordinating the anti-Cuba campaigns, and also of "Eduardo," his case officer, who in reality was none other than Howard Hunt.

They soon got started on the job and contracted Frank Sturgis, Félix Rodríguez, Bernard Baker and Eugenio Martínez (the future Watergate "plumbers") as their helpers. Their task consisted of keeping the CIA informed about the opinions and morale of the mercenaries, in order to keep them under control. The United States didn't want a repeat of the Base Trax insubordination, which could endanger their invasion plans. This group would have the job of marching behind the troops when they landed in Cuba, in order to eliminate the "communists" in the towns that were captured. They would also keep an eye on the politicians in exile and any suspicious characters who arrived from the island. In a word, they would be the ideological police of the CIA.

Within a few weeks "Sam Jenis," as he was affectionately called by the Americans, had organized his legion. He also had his own plan to assassinate Fidel. He was going to sneak Félix Rodríguez into the country, armed with a high powered rifle with

---

[39] Report from Cuban State Security.

a telescopic sight in order to shoot the leader from the top floor of a grocery store located at the corner of 11th Avenue and 12th Street in Vedado, on the block where it was assumed that the leader normally lived.

Several times during the month of January, a boat left to take Rodríguez and other agents to Varadero Beach, where their collaborators were waiting, but inclement weather and the fears of the assassins always kept their plans from materializing.

There was also another special "little job" that the group of spies had to carry out meticulously: keeping an eye on the force of 260 mercenaries that was training off the coast of South Carolina under the command of a CIA agent named Higinio Díaz Ane, a deserter from the Rebel Army. These men had been given the mission of attacking the town of Baracoa in the easternmost part of the country in order to distract the Cuban Armed Forces while the brigade landed at the Bay of Pigs. Once Baracoa had been taken, they would march to the U.S. Naval Base in Guantánamo and, pretending to be Cuban troops, simulate an attack on that installation. This plan was an ace that the CIA had up its sleeve that even President Kennedy didn't know about. They thought that this provocation could maneuver the U.S. forces there into combat in such a way that the United States government would have its hands free to act. While the details were being worked out during the month of January, Richard Bissell instructed William Harvey, who was then the Agency's chief of foreign intelligence personnel, to come up with a plan designed to create a "capability" for "executive action" designed to dissuade foreign leaders hostile to Washington's policies.

"Executive action" was a euphemism, defined by the CIA as a wide spectrum of means of "eliminating the effectiveness" of foreign leaders, with assassination being the most extreme action. This project was given the code name ZR/RIFLE.[40]

Harvey recalled years later in 1975, when testifying before a senatorial investigation into the CIA's plans to assassinate foreign leaders, that in those days Bissell had declared that on two

---

[40] *Alleged assassination plots*, 121.

separate occasions the White House had urged that such a capability be created. He also remembered that on January 25 or 26 he met with the head of the CIA laboratories, Joseph Scheider, and the case officer, Jim O'Connell, for a briefing on the attempts on the life of Fidel Castro that the two had tried months earlier. He recalled that they didn't like to use the word assassination, preferring expressions like "the last resort" and "the magic button."

At that time both Scheider and O'Connell, in collusion with the Mafia and the Cuban counterrevolution, had been involved in a plan to assassinate Fidel Castro by means of some poison pills created at the laboratory. Harvey was a man with a violent temper, and according to his own cohorts he was a classical two-gun cowboy who, when assigned to a desk job upon his return from Berlin in 1960, was at the point of turning in his resignation. Nevertheless, Bissell gave him this important task, and he went directly to the files at Langley and got the required information. Later, in his office, he carefully studied the files on foreigners linked to the CIA who were members of the underworld in their countries. He selected a few candidates who belonged to the French Mafia.

It was not difficult to contact his future collaborators, and a few days later he returned to Bissell's office with various proposals. The best method of assassination was a traitor's point-blank shot, and he proposed to his chief that they might be able to bribe someone to do that. In fact, Harvey was just following the rules of the game established many years ago by his country. How many political and business figures, or just plain ordinary citizens, had been expediently eliminated in this manner? Obviously, he didn't know the target, and when Bissell explained to him that the operation would take place in Cuba and that the object of the contract was Fidel Castro, he reconsidered his initial proposal.

He returned to his office to ponder the situation further. He reflected on the need to find men on the island who had access to the subject and, above all, the nerve to carry out the action. Without a doubt, it would be very difficult to find someone who met those conditions before events were precipitated by an invasion which everyone knew would take place in the coming weeks. He decided to wait while he formed a team with the hit men who had already been contracted, which would always be useful to the CIA.

Weeks later the Grey teams began to infiltrate through the appointed places in Cuba. One of the first was made up of Emilio Rivero Caro, Jorge García Rubio and Adolfo Mendoza, who were parachuted into Santa Cruz del Sur in Camagüey Province in March, with weapons and military stores for 25 men. Rivero's job was organizing the subversion in Pinar del Río and preparing to receive various groups of armed men who would be smuggled in through the northern coast of that region to attack the provincial capital on the day of the invasion. The other two agents were to function as radio operators for an important clandestine organization functioning in Havana, directed by Alfredo Izaguirre de la Riva and José Pujals Mederos, both of whom had been recruited by the U.S. embassy in early 1959.

In the following days the agents Pedro Rivera Castellanos, Pedro Cuéllar Alonso, Rafael García Rubio, Manuel Blanco Navarro, Javier Souto, Manuel Reyes Reyes, Segundo Borges, Jorge Rojas Castellanos, Luis Torroella, Pascasio Lineras and others were infiltrated into the country, all of whom would be captured within a few weeks.

Each had their own specific mission: Manuel Reyes was an experienced radio operator, assigned to the chief of the MRR, Rogelio González Corso. As soon as he arrived at the international airport in Havana with false papers, he was set up in a safe house in the Siboney neighborhood where he installed his radio equipment. There he became familiar with the main leaders of the cause and their differences. The daily disputes were eroding his loyalty to the cause, he noted in declarations made after he was arrested.

A different case was Jorge Rojas Castellanos, a former *casquito* and the nephew of one of Batista's generals. He had been in Guatemala and Panama and his specialty was guerrilla warfare. For these reasons he was given the job of organizing the counterrevolutionary bands in the southern part of Matanzas Province. He didn't know that this was the area that had been chosen for the invasion and that his assignment was proof of the high esteem in which he was held by the CIA. But he had bad luck there. The group which he joined, headed by Juan José Catalá Coste (alias El Pichi) stumbled into an ambush a few days after he joined them, and several of the bandits were killed. Rojas miraculously escaped and after a hazardous voyage he returned to Havana where he hid in a house in Miramar. He didn't know that he was being watched by the G-2, and that several weeks later he would be captured.

The stories of all of these "freedom fighters" are similar. Some, like Adolfo Mendoza, reconsidered as soon as they returned to their country and sought asylum in a friendly embassy; they were the lucky ones.

Meanwhile, in the Escambray mountains a decisive war was going on. Fidel Castro had disemboweled the enemy strategy of converting this region into the rear guard of the counterrevolution. Beginning in the final months of 1960, he organized a military operation known as *La Limpia del Escambray* (the Escambray Cleanup), in which tens of thousands of militia from all over the country joined the Rebel Army in wiping out the counterrevolutionary bands one by one.

In January and February 1961, the revolutionary forces captured a number of arms and supply shipments which the CIA had sent to its guerrillas for use in support of the invasion. On January 6, a plane dropped in the Condado area, near the city of Trinidad, a 57 millimeter cannon with 16 projectiles; 3 bazookas with 45 projectiles; two 60 millimeter mortars with 60 shells; 60 Springfield submachine guns; 5 machine guns with 9,100 rounds of ammunition; 72 fragmentation grenades; 4 boxes of fuses, detonators and high-powered explosives; 4 portable radios; and quantities of batteries, medicines, etc. Not long afterwards, on February 6, another plane launched various parachutes with weapons and equipment into the Santa Lucía zone, in the municipality of Cabaiguán.

Luis Felipe Denis Díaz was the G-2 official that the revolutionary command sent to penetrate and break up the counterrevolutionary groups. He and his group of young officers worked arduously to complete this task, which they knew was vital for the defense of the nation. In the process, they learned to work with the intelligence, astuteness and intransigence that this silent war requires. Many of them were killed in the line of duty, and history has recorded their names and the undying memory of their example.

On March 4, Fidel Castro, in a commemorative activity for the first anniversary of the sabotage of the ship *La Coubre*, informed the people of the elimination of the greater part of the bands that had tried to convert the Escambray mountains into a beachhead of imperialism. Thirty-nine bandits had been killed and 381 captured in the most recent operations. The enemy's plan was coming unraveled. This news weighed heavily on the leaders of the CIA's task force. In recent months they had been working on the idea of using those subversive forces to isolate and blockade the southern city of Trinidad which, nestled between the spurs of that mountain range and the shores of the undulating beaches, offered the perfect setting for the disembarkation of the mercenary troops. They could then occupy the city and bring in their provisional government, made up of the Cuban Revolutionary Council (CRC), which would then solicit military aid from the United States.

Faced with the failure of the plan, the CIA brains turned to their colleagues in the Pentagon to look for other options. That is how Operation Zapata came into being, elaborated by military officials who proposed that the scene of the mercenary landing be switched to the Bay of Pigs on the Zapata Peninsula in the southern part of Matanzas Province.[41] There was a small airport, and the basic conditions for a force such as the one they were preparing to take a beachhead and, due to the inaccessibility of the terrain, to hold it until the U.S. Armed Forces entered the conflict.

---

[41] *30 años*, Operation Zapata.

During the night of March 13, Sorí Marín, Díaz Hanscom and Grey team members Manuel Puig Miyar, Nemesio Rodríguez Navarrete and Gaspar Domingo Trueba Varona, armed and equipped with nearly two tons of explosives, sneaked onto the beach at Celimar, near the capital. The boat was driven by Aldo Vera and Albertico Fernández, who wisely returned to their burrow after they dropped off the others. The idea was to instigate the plan proposed to Howard Hunt and approved by the CIA: assassinate Fidel Castro, unite the counterrevolutionary groups, and unleash a terrorist campaign that would intimidate the population.

The infiltrators had little time, and although each took a separate path to avoid suspicion, they agreed to meet in a safe house at 9:00 p.m. on March 18, along with Rogelio González Corso and other counterrevolutionary leaders, to sign the unity agreement among the organizations which the CIA had previously authorized.

The day came, and visitors began to arrive at the house, located at 110 186th Street in the Siboney neighborhood. They were unaware that the G-2 knew about the conclave and that for several months the movements of Sorí Marín and the others had been closely monitored. Most of the counterrevolutionary groups that the conspirators thought they could rely on had already been penetrated. Thus a "rebellion" was staged by Captain Alcibiades Bermúdez and a group of his comrades in order to infiltrate Sorí Marín's group and give the impression that a large band of outlaws operated in the Sierra de los Organos. The "Eastern Bandits" were also revolutionary infiltrators into the ranks of the counterrevolutionary organizations. Moreover, almost all of the conspirators in the Navy and the police stations were closely watched, and it was not difficult to round them up when the time came.

When everyone had arrived at the house and the scrambling over control of the new unit being formed was at its height, the G-2 gate-crashed the party and confiscated the plans, maps, outline and of course, the weapons and explosives designed to terrorize the population.

A quick glance at the documents demonstrated that the so-called Front for Revolutionary Unity was made up of 28 organizations, and its leadership composed of Varona's man, Rafael Díaz Hanscom, the coordinator; Sorí Marín, the military chief; Rogelio González Corso, the delegate from the FRD; Marcial Arufe, in charge of supplies; Salvador García, manager of the finances; with Bebo Borrón and Antonio Díaz directing the propaganda; and Manuel Puig, Manuel Reyes Reyes and other radio operators controlling the communications.

Forty bundles of a very powerful explosive were picked up on the beach at Celimar, along with incendiary devices, detonating fuses, plastic explosives, and weapons of various kinds. The arrests made, which the counterrevolutionaries attributed for many years to coincidence, were a serious blow to the diversionary plans orchestrated by the CIA to arm and train the fifth column which was supposed to clear the way for the Bay of Pigs mercenaries. The principal leaders were captured in the following days, and as the other aspects of the scheme were revealed, the conspirators' hideouts began to fall into the hands of Cuban State Security.

Howard Hunt and James Noel were concerned when they heard of the arrests in Cuba. An urgent meeting was called in the crisis room of the CIA offices in Miami. Present were the principal architects of espionage involved in the Cuban case. Tracy Barnes couldn't hide his uneasiness, in spite of his efforts to do so. He sat at the head of the table in an elegant gray suit, with his sparse hair combed neatly. On his right were Hunt, Phillips, Noel Bender and other members of the CIA's inner circles. On his left were several Cubans, trusted agents who had come to report on the mishap. Aldo Vera was the first to speak. In the end, with his characteristic dramatic style, he proposed a risky plan to salvage the situation. The North Americans looked at each other. They could not inform the Kennedy administration, for surely the President would cancel the operation, with all that it implied.

Barnes had spoken the previous afternoon with Bissell and they both agreed on how important it was to land the mercenaries in Cuba, whatever the price. They even accepted the Pentagon's latest proposal that the new site be the Zapata Swamp, because they wanted the military as their ally. They thought the United States would inevitably have to intervene to save the mercenaries or it would lose face, and no president, not even Kennedy, could afford that.

Aldo Vera was invited to explain his plan, which consisted of infiltrating two of their best men through Punto Fundora into a place called Palmarejo, on the border between Havana and Matanzas. Once in Cuba, they would contact a counter-revolutionary group that had escaped capture, and together they would organize the rescue of Sorí Marín and his friends from the G-2 building on Fifth Avenue and 14th Street in the Miramar neighborhood. In this case, Aldo Vera's bravado was not the fatal flaw. It was the fact that his masters believed him and, full of hope, authorized him to carry out the operation.

On the night of March 29, a boat belonging to Albertico Fernández, under the command of Aldo Vera, who stayed aboard as usual, cast anchor at the prearranged place. Braulio Contreras Mazo and Angel Posada Gutiérrez (known as Polín) slipped out quickly into the maze of mangroves. They spent the night in the beach town of Guanabo, near the capital. There they made their first mistake: they left behind two pistols, which were immediately reported to the G-2.

Braulio Contreras had two additional tasks: turn over 60,000 Cuban pesos to the new leader of the Front for Revolutionary Unity, which was to take over and organize a wave of sabotage and terror in Havana. Their priorities included arson at the Sears, La Epoca, Flogar and El Encanto department stores. It was during the sabotage of the latter that the exemplary revolutionary Fe del Valle perished.

At the law office on the corner of Aguiar and Empedrado, Contreras was eagerly awaited. Attorney Ernesto Betancourt was the new treasurer of the Frente, and he was to receive the money sent by the CIA. From him Contreras learned that various conspirators — headed by Carlos Bandín, Alfredo Izaguirre, José Pujals, Antonio Borrón and Roberto Guedes — had eluded capture by the revolutionary authorities, and were regrouping the few counterrevolutionary structures that hadn't been dismantled. After explaining the missions assigned him by the CIA, Contreras asked for help in the planned rescue, and was given the use of a residence at the strategic corner of First Avenue and 12th Street, only a few dozen meters from the G-2 offices.

The plan consisted of dressing in olive green Rebel Army officers' uniforms and then arriving in the early hours of the morning when it was assumed that the G-2 chiefs would be asleep. They had managed to obtain false papers authorizing the transfer of Sorí Marín and the others to Las Cabañas Prison, a maximum security unit where the most dangerous prisoners were usually detained. Once they had safely spirited away the prisoners, they would communicate with the CIA center in Miami and Aldo Vera would collect them at the appointed spot on the coast. Everything seemed simple. What they didn't foresee, however, was that Cuban State Security knew of their plans and they were arrested just a few days before the expected invasion.

Meanwhile, in the United States, the operation to assassinate Fidel Castro was well under way. The Agency's laboratories had produced capsules filled with a powerful poison, a synthetic botulism, which took effect a few hours after it was administered, giving the mafiosos time to make their escape. In early March, John Rosselli communicated to Jim O'Connell at the CIA through his contact Maheu that the capsules had been delivered to the Cuban official Juan Orta Córdova, who was employed in the Prime Minister's office. But the criminal did not have the nerve to act. He was dissuaded by the security measures surrounding Fidel, and a few days later asked for exile in a Latin American embassy to await the announced invasion.

Rosselli informed O'Connell of the failure, but also told him that Santos Trafficante, another Miami mafioso, was close to a figure in the Cuban exile movement who could carry out the crime. His contact was the well-known Tony Varona, Trafficante's old collaborator in the gambling, prostitution and drug businesses in pre-revolutionary Cuba. In the 1950s they had also formed a corporation together called ANSAN which, through extortion, had bought up property very cheaply in South Florida. The contribution of Varona, who was president of the Cuban Senate at the time, was to provide protection for the mafiosos on the island.

Trafficante's proposal to Varona was simple: use the men in his organization to assassinate Fidel Castro in exchange for a million dollars and the security of the crime syndicate in their new business which they would set up again in Cuba once the revolution was destroyed. Varona had a man in the Pekín Restaurant whom he happily placed under the orders of the Mafia. The plan was quickly put together. The capsules would be given to someone who worked at the restaurant who could then carry it out as soon as Fidel dined there.

The money and the capsules were turned over to Varona at a meeting with Rosselli and Trafficante at the Hotel Fountainebleau in Miami on March 12, 1961. According to testimony by Rosselli before a U.S. Senate select committee investigating assassination plots against foreign leaders, the meeting went like this:

> [Robert Maheu] opened his briefcase and dumped a whole lot of money on his lap. . . and also came up with the capsules and he explained how they were going to be used. As far as I remember, they couldn't be used in boiling soups and things like that, but they could be used in water or otherwise, but they couldn't last forever. . . It had to be done as quickly as possible. [42]

Nevertheless, Joseph Shimon, a friend of Rosselli and Giancana who was also present at the meeting when the money and capsules were handed over, had another version. He recalled a long conversation with Maheu, who assured him that a "contract" had been taken out on Fidel and that the CIA had provided a liquid to be mixed in his food, adding that he would die within two or three days and that an autopsy would reveal nothing.

---

[42] *Alleged assassination plots*, 81-82

Shimon added that Maheu had said, "Johnny's going to handle everything; this is Johnny's contract," adding that the delayed action of the poison would allow the perpetrator to flee before the appearance of the first symptoms.

Actually, the plan was carried out somewhat differently. In late February 1961, Tony Varona sent a message to his lieutenant in Havana, the counterrevolutionary Alberto Cruz Caso, head of the Rescate Movement, telling him to send someone he could trust to Miami. The contact selected was Rodolfo León Curbelo, Varona's old pal who had earned Alberto Cruz' complete confidence. Once in Miami, Curbelo met with Varona who gave him the capsules and a letter with detailed written instructions for the unit in Havana. In the letter, he emphasized that Fidel was to be assassinated only after the order was given by telephone. The CIA had expressly stated that they wanted to coordinate the assassination with the planned invasion. Varona also requested that he be contacted by phone once the action had been carried out. He wanted to deliver this surprise to the American authorities, and thus recoup his lost power.

When he returned to the island's capital, Curbelo gave the capsules and the instructions to Cruz Caso and María Leopoldina Grau Alsina, who quickly met with the employee of the Pekín Restaurant, located on busy 23rd Street, near the corner of 14th, in Vedado. But the order never arrived. The CIA, in its eagerness to hide complicity in the crime, had not bothered to learn the name of "the Cuban" to whom the Mafia had given the contract, and therefore, when they rounded up all of the members of the Cuban Revolutionary Council for safekeeping a few days before the invasion, Tony Varona was among them.

When the case officer, Jim O'Connell, phoned Robert Maheu to give the Mafia the green light, Trafficante couldn't find Varona, who was sequestered in a CIA safe house. So, the order was never given; but even if it had been, the criminal plans of the would-be assassins would not have been successful. The Cuban G-2 had already taken the necessary precautions, and the security of the head of the revolution was assured.

Nor was the revolution taken by surprise on April 17, 1961, when the mercenary brigade landed at the Bay of Pigs. The political leadership, headed by Commander in Chief Fidel Castro, had carefully prepared the defense that the militia and the Rebel Army would use in the imminent battle. This was the main reason why the diversionary landings in Pinar del Río and Baracoa were not effective. Fidel held back his forces to use them against the main attack, and as soon as he learned that the Bay of Pigs landing had taken place, he ordered them deployed.

The 160 men trained in New Orleans never had the courage to reach the beach in Baracoa. They only prowled the coast, and when they learned that revolutionary troops were marching down the highway toward the town they expected to take, they turned their boat around and headed for the Bay of Pigs, where they arrived too late.

The hoax failed, and in spite of the bombing of our airports in an attempt to destroy the country's airforce, and the landing of the brigade in a remote area of the Zapata Peninsula, thousands of combatants soon converged on the area, and defeated the mercenaries within a few hours.

This was without a doubt one of the most glorious pages in the history of revolutionary battles and of the Cuban people, along with the silent war which the men and women of Cuban State Security waged alongside the people against the fifth column which waited anxiously for the moment to attack from the rear. Hundreds of acts of sabotage, planned assassinations and incidents of terrorism were aborted. The capture of tens of thousands of counterrevolutionaries throughout the country by the population-turned-militia was certainly one of the determining factors in the April 19 victory.

CHAPTER 6

The empire strikes back: Operations Patty and Liborio

After the defeat at the Bay of Pigs, the internal counterrevolution, encouraged by the U.S. government, began almost immediately to regroup to carry out a new campaign of terrorism and psychological warfare. This campaign was to have culminated on July 26, 1961, with the assassination of Commanders Fidel Castro and Raúl Castro and a simultaneous provocation at the U.S. Naval Base in Guantánamo, initiating a conflict between the two countries and the pretext for an open military intervention by U.S. troops, which would be ready and waiting at military bases in the southern United States.

It was an operation which the CIA had been developing since 1959, and which they considered an alternative to Sorí Marín's conspiracy. The groups involved in these plans had salvaged their forces from the Bay of Pigs debacle and had highly trusted agents, including Alfredo Izaguirre de la Riva, Luis Torroella, José Pujals, and Octavio Barroso. These elements were divided into three groups: one which operated in the former Oriente Province, and the other two in the nation's capital. The CIA immediately launched its attack. It wanted to demonstrate to Kennedy that, despite the defeat it had suffered, the Cuban question could still be resolved and the empire could save face.

In early May 1961, CIA agent AM/BLOOD, working out of Santiago de Cuba, sent the following message in secret writing to an address in Quito, the capital of Ecuador:

Political situation: the sentiments of both sides deepening since May 1. The declaration of the socialist state, the restriction of liberties, the firing squads, the attacks on the Church have all been received by the Cubans with silent resentment. The failure at the Bay of Pigs has caused confusion and desperation, but now they are beginning to act again. The absence of internal orientation and action is impeding the civil resistance activity. The Council of Miró Cardona, who is a very respected man, doesn't give the public the inspiration they need. In reality they don't identify with the people. They are only figureheads and not leaders. That is the reason why there is no open opposition. The economic situation is quite serious. The scarcity of products from abroad is great, and there is a lack of those produced domestically as well. The people are expressing their complaints more openly. The sugar harvest is almost finished. It was successful, but the sugar hasn't been sold, it's piled up in warehouses. The molasses hasn't been sold either, and they have had to throw out a large part of it for lack of warehouse space. Stop, stop, stop.[43]

On May 10, AM/BLOOD received a response, also in code:

Message number six: Luis, received your messages three and four. Both well developed. Please continue regularly sending reports on the situation in Cuba in invisible ink. We are particularly interested in the following: morale and attitude of the friendly groups, the actual force of these groups and the possibility and probability of internal insurrection in the future in case material aid were to be sent. If the failure of

---

[43] Messages confiscated by the G-2. Cuban State Security files. May 1961.

the invasion has really reinforced Castro's control in Cuba, the public's reaction in that case; the means of vigilance and security; some indications of disaffection in the working class and the lower classes. Luis, I propose you use the radio to only send urgent messages in order to maintain your security, which is the most important thing. Inform position of the other members of the intelligence network. Basilio. Stop, stop, stop.[44]

AM/BLOOD's mission consisted of coordinating the actions of the counterrevolutionary organizations in the eastern provinces that had survived the Bay of Pigs. He had been infiltrated and properly outfitted for the purpose of stirring up a rebellion in the major cities of that region and establishing various guerrilla bands that would devastate the countryside. His groups were to create instability that would lead up to the principal action: the provocation at the Guantánamo Naval Base.

In Havana, some of the counterrevolutionaries who had escaped justice tried to stabilize their few remaining structures and reestablish links with their U.S. contacts. For the latter, they decided to send an emissary to Miami. They selected Alfredo Izaguirre de la Riva, a journalist and descendant of one of the wealthiest and most powerful Havana families. He had been recruited by the CIA to organize the internal front on the eve of the invasion, and only by coincidence had escaped being arrested along with Sorí Marín and company, having missed the meeting because he was not at home when the messenger came to tell him about it. He was discouraged and had suggested that the counterrevolution was finished, adding that he was ready to go to the United States soon to reorganize his life. Perhaps that was why he was commissioned for this trip, so that he could meet with the CIA chiefs and they could explain to him what was happening, and then he could decide on his future plans. He took advantage of the fact that his papers were in order and left for

---

[44] Report from the G-2 Information Department of Oriente Province on CIA agent Luis Torroella y Martín Rivero.

Miami, where he met with various case officers, among them David Phillips and Jack Esterline. He found, according to later statements, a generalized demoralization. "Everyone damned the Kennedy brothers, while bitterly lamenting the luck of Brigade 2506." [45]

After several meetings in Miami, he decided to travel to Washington to meet with a CIA agent in charge of the Cuban case. There he was received by Frank Bender who, after a few conversations to feel him out, informed him of the existence of the Taylor Commission, charged by President Kennedy with investigating the Bay of Pigs disaster. Days later he was taken to the Pentagon, to an office with General Maxwell Taylor's name on it. Inside were several persons, in addition to the general himself. The conversation turned into a long interrogatory session. The men assembled there wanted to know the impact of the Bay of Pigs fiasco on the Cuban population, and above all the state of the counterrevolution and the prospects of mobilizing it once again. In one of the exchanges, he was asked, "How many men are in Manuel Ray's People's Revolutionary Movement?"

Izaguirre responded that there were around seven hundred.

"We calculate two hundred," responded the questioner.

"There may be two hundred, or there may be seven hundred, but not even with all of the men in all of the clandestine organizations in Cuba can the government be toppled," Izaguirre replied.

"We agree with your assessment, but the Cubans should get the idea out of their heads that the Marines will come in cold to resolve the Cuban problem. It depends on you to create a situation to propitiate direct aid."

"What chance is there of promoting a general uprising on the island?" he was asked. "Such an action would justify our intervention in the eyes of the world. Another justification might be if the Cuban government — or somebody — attacked the Guantánamo Naval Base."

---

[45] Declarations by Alfredo Izaguirre de la Riva to Cuban State Security. July 1961.

Later, in the privacy of his hotel room, Izaguirre confided to Frank Bender his impressions of the meeting. "I understand that the United States needs a pretext to intervene militarily in Cuba, and I assure you that we won't fail them. The Naval Base will be attacked and you can blame Castro for this act. . . ."[46]

Toward the end of May, Izaguirre returned to Havana with new instructions and, above all, the guarantee that the United States would back them up with material and financial resources. Among the first tasks to be undertaken was uniting the counterrevolutionary leaders, since the defeat had caused many schisms. Even one of the CIA agents with whom he worked, José Pujals Mederos, was maneuvering behind his back for support among the conspirators to go to the United States and have Izaguirre removed from the position given him by the Agency.

Another of the obstacles to be overcome was that inside the Italian embassy, where some of the leaders who had escaped the April arrests had sought asylum, a Junta of Counterrevolutionary Unity had been formed which demanded recognition by the battered Democratic Revolutionary Council, the screen used by the CIA to direct its subversive activities against Cuba.

After many discussions — in which the secret agents of the Cuban G-2 also participated — a single structure was created which, ignoring the claims of those inside the Italian embassy, proclaimed itself the legitimate heir of the Front for Revolutionary Unity, dismantled on the eve of the Bay of Pigs. The leadership of the newly-created coordinating group was given to Carlos Bandín, a leader of the MRR, and the other positions were divided up among representatives of the participating organizations: the November 30 Movement, the Christian Democratic Movement, the People's Revolutionary Movement, Revolutionary Unity, and several others. Izaguirre and Pujals reserved for themselves the job of serving as CIA contacts. Their radio operator, Jorge García Rubio, worked long days transmitting the latest news and receiving new instructions, some

---

[46] Declarations by Izaguirre.

of which pinpointed the spots where parachutes would be dropped with the promised materials.

In early June, Izaguirre, Pujals and Bandín reviewed the progress of their plans. In Oriente Province, they had reestablished communications with an important group that was in constant contact with the Naval Base at Guantánamo; in Camagüey, a branch of the Democratic Insurrectional Movement (MID) had arms and explosives, and, even more important, they were willing to take part in the planned actions. In Las Villas, CIA agent Javier Souto and an MRR group had been able to contact the bandit leader Osvaldo Ramírez, who operated in the Escambray, and he agreed to coordinate his activities with the new front. Rivero Caro, another of the spies who had been sent to the island, had reorganized his Cuba Libre (Free Cuba) group in Pinar del Río.

And so the structure began to be created for one of the most important and dangerous operations carried out by the CIA against the Cuban revolution: the one code named "Patty."[47]

The project contemplated actions throughout the country for the purpose of propagating a conflict and encouraging the general uprising that Washington had ordered. The main activities were supposed to take place in the cities of Havana and Santiago de Cuba, where simultaneous celebrations were being held on July 26. In the eastern capital, the plan consisted of taking by assault one of the houses adjoining the place where Commander Raúl Castro was supposed to speak and installing a 30 caliber machine gun there with which to shoot the revolutionary leader. Four men armed with grenades would then cover the escape of the assassins. In addition, an ambush by six men armed with submachine guns was arranged for the highway leading from the city to the airport, so that in case Raúl Castro escaped from the public meeting unharmed, he could be killed as he prepared to board the plane to return to Havana.

The actions were scheduled to begin at 10:00 in the morning, and to be synchronized with a mortar attack on the oil refinery.

---

[47] *30 años*, Operation Patty-Candela.

At the same time, from a farm called El Cuero, near the U.S. Naval Base, a battery of no less than four mortars would be fired toward the installation, while another mortar would be fired at the nearby Cuban military installation, so that both sides would think they were being attacked and a generalized combat would ensue.

At the same time, the counterrevolutionaries in Havana had hidden an 82 millimeter mortar in the vicinity of Revolution Square from which they would fire in the direction of the podium where Fidel Castro and the majority of revolutionary leaders were present at the celebration. That same day, the groups that had been armed and organized in the provinces would begin their planned actions against the major public services and bridges in their respective regions. The plan included the elimination of leading revolutionaries, in such a way that within a few hours after launching Operation Patty, the chaos and destabilization generated would create the proper conditions for a U.S. military invasion.

In late June, the conspiracy's radio operator, Jorge García Rubio, transmitted the final details of the plan, and received approval from the CIA center, as well as precise instructions for coordinating the supply of weapons and military materials destined for groups operating throughout the country. On July 12, José Pujals Mederos slipped out of the country to Miami, for the purpose of reporting in detail on the progress of Operation Patty, doing a little politicking for his own interests, and receiving his instructions.

AM/BLOOD, who operated in Santiago de Cuba, was arrested. Years later, Philip Agee admitted being the person in the CIA's Quito office who received the messages sent by AM/BLOOD, whose identity was Luis Torroella y Martín Rivero.

While the Central Intelligence Agency was entangled in Operation Patty, the government commission headed by General Maxwell Taylor which had been created to look into the causes of the failure of the Bay of Pigs invasion, concluded its analysis. Among its conclusions were the following:

We have been struck with the general feeling that there can be no long-term living with Castro as a neighbor. His continued presence within the hemispheric community as a dangerously effective exponent of Communism and Anti-Americanism constitutes a real menace capable of eventually overthrowing the elected governments in any one or more of [the] weak Latin American republics. [48]

He added that he was personally inclined to follow a positive line of action against Castro, recognizing the danger of treating the Cuban problem outside the context of the Cold War. He recommended that the Cuban situation be reevaluated in the light of all the factors known at the time, to thus obtain a new guideline for propaganda, political, economic and military actions.

On July 22, Cuban State Security forces detained Operation Patty's principal plotters and confiscated their weapons and military supplies. A fragment of the information obtained by the G-2 in Oriente Province when they dismantled the subversive plans illustrates the complexity and importance of this operation:

One of the counterrevolutionary leaders, José Amparo Rosabal, alias El Zorro, was sheltered at the Yankee naval base coordinating the plans. . . . he was head of the provincial delegation of the Ministry of Transportation in the early days of the revolution and an old collaborator of Carlos Prío and Tony Varona, connected to the CIA through the agent Nino Díaz who was linked to the intelligence service at the base. . . . The plan consisted of leaving the weapons outside the fence of the aforementioned installation on the morning of July 17. Those responsible for retrieving the armaments were Antonio Marra Acosta and Emilio Quintana González, who were to arrive at the appointed place in a jeep and pick

---

[48] Taylor, *Memorandum No. 4 Recommendations of the Cuban Study Group.*

them up. . . . Waiting for them there was a North American sergeant named Smith, the person who would hand over the armaments. At the time of their arrest, the following weapons were taken from the aforementioned counterrevolutionaries: two 57 millimeter cannons, four bazookas, 23 Garand rifles and sufficient ammunition and hand grenades to carry out the plans.

Later other arms that had been turned over by the Yankee base were also seized, including 35 Springfield rifles; one 60 millimeter mortar; one 30 caliber machine gun; 12 M-3 submachine guns; two M-1 carbines and ammunition, and the grenades and explosives needed for their operations . . . [49]

The Cuban government publicly denounced to the world this latest planned aggression which had been completely dismantled.

After the failure of Operation Patty, the CIA took stock of their losses. They still had the People's Revolutionary Movement (MRP), which was carrying out plans parallel to Operation Patty. One of the first agents recruited in 1959 was a militant member of that organization: Antonio Veciana Blanch, a public accountant who had worked for the sugar magnate Julio Lobo during the final years of the Batista dictatorship. The revolution spoiled his rising career in the world of finance, and this was the opportunity that CIA official David Phillips took advantage of to recruit him. In the final months of 1959, Veciana was trained in the techniques of sabotage, terrorism, espionage and psychological warfare. He was among the first to join the MRP, founded by Manuel Ray. This organization tried to attract dissidents from the revolutionary ranks with a demagogical program that called for retaining the social measures taken by the revolution, but without socialism, as if the two were not inherently linked.

The MRP soon fell into disgrace when Manuel Ray fled to the United States during the final days of 1960. There he joined José Miró Cardona's Cuban Revolutionary Council, but the CIA

---

[49] Report from the Cuban State Security Department of Oriente Province on Operation Patty-Candela, 1961.

and the counterrevolutionaries with a longer-term perspective mistrusted his "socializing" discourse.

After the Bay of Pigs fiasco there was a great purge in the political ranks in exile, and Manuel Ray was one of those who fell into disgrace. It was part of the cost of the defeat. The organization in Cuba also had its purges, and those close to Ray were replaced. Ignacio Mendoza was designated as the new representative of the organization in the United States, and Reynold González was made the head of the group on the island, with Antonio Veciana as his right-hand man.

In early 1961, the CIA had ordered Veciana to study the Presidential Palace. That was the place where public meetings were held and Fidel Castro generally addressed the crowd from the north terrace of the building. Veciana patiently checked out all of the apartments in the vicinity until he found the one that he needed, situated at No. 29 Avenida de las Misiones, apartment 8A, some 50 meters from the podium. With the same meticulousness, various weapons were brought into the apartment, among them the bazooka which was supposed to be used for the assassination. When Operation Patty was set in motion, the CIA already had this alternative plan to assassinate Fidel in case of a last minute change of venue for the mass gathering scheduled for Revolution Square.

Izaguirre and his associates were arrested, but the CIA still had one card left, and they decided to play it. CIA officials "Harold Bishop" and Frank Bender met with agent José Pujals, who had been in Washington when he was caught unawares by the Operation Patty setback. Pujals was ordered to assume command of the CIA agents on the island and particularly to determine the state of the MRP's plans, as well as to assess the damage done to the group. If everything was normal, he was to coordinate an operation whose code name would be Liborio, which would include assassinating the Cuban leader, launching an extensive sabotage and terrorism campaign, and orchestrating, in conjunction with the Catholic hierarchy, a psychological warfare project designed to discredit the revolution in the eyes of the people. In this way they would take the offensive once again and finally achieve the destabilization that would permit the long-awaited military intervention.

Pujals arrived in the capital in late July 1961, after a risky voyage in which the CIA infiltrated him back into the country along the coast north of Havana. A few days later he met with Reynold González, Veciana and the spy Octavio Barroso, and explained to them the plan as instructed by his CIA controllers. The idea was to ignite Havana — to burn down the big clothing stores and the electrical and transportation facilities — and at the same time to assassinate various leaders of revolutionary organizations. This would provoke public indignation, and surely end in a mass demonstration in front of the Presidential Palace which could be the opportunity to assassinate Fidel. At the same time they would coordinate with the Catholic hierarchy the dissemination of a copy of a supposed Patria Potestad law, which they themselves would write, saying that the State was going to take away parents' power over their children. The conspiring priests would then proceed to spread the lie from their pulpits, in such a way that the population, eminently religious, would challenge the revolution and thus create the internal conditions which, together with the physical elimination of Fidel, would produce the fall of the government.

On August 8, Pujals and Barroso were arrested by Cuban security forces, who, after having been alerted by their collaborators of the presence of the spies, captured them in Barroso's home. Days later, the G-2 learned the most important aspects of the operation and commenced to take protective measures, while continuing an exhaustive investigation to uncover all of the details of the plot.

On September 29, Dalia Jorge Díaz was caught in the act of planting an incendiary device in the Sears store. In her statements, she explained the following:

> I had arrived at the store at 5:45 p.m., and I went directly to the second floor where there was a table of decorator fabrics. I inserted the envelope which contained the incendiary device and then went directly to the ground floor to plant

the second device in the place that had been indicated . . .
This action formed part of the so-called Operation Liborio,
which consisted of a series of synchronized acts of sabotage
on the same day and time, in order to set Havana on fire.[50]

October 4 had been chosen as the day to carry out the attempt on
the Cuban leader's life. The national press had reported in detail
on the visit of Cuban President Osvaldo Dorticós to the Soviet
Union, and the masses in the capital had been convoked to
welcome him back that day in the area around the Presidential
Palace. Veciana, in complicity with Reynold González, alerted
the men who had been chosen for the assassination. After firing
the bazooka at the podium, they were to toss several grenades
indiscriminately into the crowd and then, dressed in militia
uniforms, they could flee under the cover of the chaos.

On his own initiative, Veciana had taken several precautions
in case there were difficulties with the operation or if one of the
plotters were caught and confessed. He had a fisherman waiting
for him on a nearby beach with a boat ready to take him north.
The arrest of Dalia Jorge precipitated the stampede. Frightened,
Veciana fled on October 3, abandoning the rest of his men to fate.
As soon as the group of assassins heard the news of the flight of
their leader, they fled the apartment at full gallop and each of
them, including the leaders of the organization, sought refuge in
different hiding places they were sure the G-2 didn't know about.

Within a few days, all of them had been arrested, their
weapons confiscated and Cuban deunciations were once again
hammered out on teletypes throughout the world. However, very
few people got to hear Cuba's story since the international media
monopolies blocked the news.

Juan Manuel Izquierdo Díaz, one of Veciana's lieutenants in
the murderous plans, declared shortly after his arrest:

---

[50] Declarations by Dalia Jorge Díaz to Cuban State Security. October
1961.

I was told that a series of jobs was being prepared in conjunction with people from other movements, such as carrying out sabotage in Havana and Santiago. The attempt on Fidel in the Palace was the main action and for this it was necessary to insure a way out for the woman who was the owner of the apartment on Misiones Street . . . [51]

On October 11, on a farm in Wajay, an area situated just outside the city of Havana, Reynold González, the MRP's top man, was captured along with a group of his collaborators. He spoke at a televised news conference to inform the public of the details of Operation Liborio. Among the essential aspects he cited were:

In effect, when President Dorticós left for the socialist countries, the military section of our movement, commanded by Veciana, who had an apartment in front of the Presidential Palace, planned an attempt against Fidel and the other leaders. At that time we had a bazooka and everything necessary in the apartment. When Dorticós' return was announced, the plans were concretized, including the burning of the main department stores in Havana, such as Sears, J. Vallés, Fin de Siglo and others. There were 15 in all. . . . this failed because the people's guard in the stores detained the persons who had this mission . . . . in spite of this, the act was held in the Palace, and incomprehensibly for us, the main organizer of the action, Antonio Veciana, fled to Miami in a boat the day before. The attempt was not carried out, and now the apartment and the equipment is in the hands of the State Security Department. . . . [52]

Thus concluded the adventures of the CIA in the year 1961, in which they tried to topple the Cuban revolution by means of a mercenary invasion and covert warfare. Thousands of saboteurs,

---

[51] Declarations by Juan Manuel Izquierdo Díaz. Cuban State Security files. October 1961.

[52] Declarations by Reynold González González, head of the MRP. Cuban State Security files. October 1961.

terrorists and spies were captured; tons of arms and matériel were confiscated; and most significantly, the counterrevolution failed to form a fifth column that would have undermined the revolutionary rear guard and facilitated the assassination of the head of the Cuban revolution.

CHAPTER 7

Operation Mongoose

On November 30, 1961, after analyzing the report of the Taylor Commission on the failure of the mercenary Bay of Pigs invasion, the National Security Council created a special committee, charged by President John F. Kennedy with overthrowing the revolutionary Cuban government. This committee was called the Special Group (Augmented) [SGA].

This task force created and approved within a year a new phase of the covert war which, under the code name of Mongoose, united the efforts of various U.S. government agencies to try once more to topple the revolution. Believing that the end justifies the means, they favored a well-planned general uprising, the assassination of Fidel Castro, and a campaign to discredit the revolution in Latin America, using all available resources.

The Special Group (Augmented) included the regular members of the Special Group (CIA Director John McCone, National Security Adviser McGeorge Bundy, Alexis Johnson of the State Department, Roswell Gilpatric of the Defense Department, and General Lyman L. Lemnitzer of the Joint Chiefs of Staff) with the addition of Attorney General Robert Kennedy and General Maxwell Taylor, who would later become chairman of the Joint Chiefs of Staff of the Armed Forces. Although Secretary of State Dean Rusk and Secretary of Defense

Robert McNamara were not formally members of either of the two groups, they sometimes participated in the meetings.[53]

Instead of designating Robert Kennedy chairman of the group as had been proposed, General Edward Lansdale, an officer experienced in counterinsurgency warfare in the Philippines and Vietnam, was selected to head up Operation Mongoose. However, on October 4, 1962, the group decided that Robert Kennedy should chair its meetings "for the time being."[54] The fact is that Robert Kennedy played a very active role in Operation Mongoose, seemingly far removed from his responsibilities as Attorney General.

In that same month of November 1961, the CIA had appointed William Harvey head of its Operation Mongoose task force (Task Force W). He had previously been head of ZR/RIFLE, created a few days before John F. Kennedy assumed the presidency, for the purpose of creating the capability to eliminate inconvenient foreign political leaders.[55]

At the end of December 1961, General Lansdale formed a task force composed of representatives from the CIA, the Pentagon, the State Department and the United States Information Agency (USIA). This task force was to direct the anti-Cuba operation under orders from President Kennedy. Its mission consisted of coordinating and controlling, in the name of the Special Group (Augmented), the plans approved by all of the government agencies involved in the program. Lansdale was given an office in the Pentagon and he immediately set to work.

The first plan elaborated for the consideration of the U.S. leaders was submitted on January 18, 1962, and it proposed, among other measures, the following:

[53] *Alleged assassination plots*, 140.
[54] *Alleged assassination plots*, 147, note 2.
[55] Inspector General J.S. Earman, *Memorandum for the record. Report on plots to assassinate Fidel Castro*, May 23, 1967, 38-39. Published in 1995 by Ocean Press as *CIA targets Fidel.*

The U.S. objective is to help the Cubans overthrow the Communist regime from within Cuba and institute a new government with which the United States can live in peace.

Basically, the operation is to bring about the revolt of the Cuban people . . . . The revolt requires a strongly motivated political action movement established within Cuba, to generate the revolt, to give it direction towards the objective and to capitalize on the climactic moment. The political actions will be assisted by economic warfare to induce failure of the Communist regime to supply Cuba's economic needs, psychological operations to turn the peoples' resentment increasingly against the regime, and military-type groups to give the popular movement an action arm for sabotage and armed resistance in support of political objectives. . . .

The preparation phase must result in a political action organization in being in [sic] key localities inside Cuba, with its own means for internal communications, its own voice for psychological operations, and its own action arm (small guerrilla bands, sabotage squads etc.). It must have the sympathetic support of the majority of the Cuban people, and make this fact known to the outside world. . . .

The climactic moment of revolt will come from an angry reaction of the people to a government action (sparked by an incident), or from a fracturing of the leadership cadre within the regime, or both. . . .

The popular movement will capitalize on this climactic moment by initiating an open revolt. Areas will be taken and held. If necessary, the popular movement will appeal for help to the free nations of the Western Hemisphere. The United States, if possible in concert with other Western Hemisphere nations, will then give open support to the Cuban peoples' revolt. Such support will include military force, as necessary.[56]

---

[56] Brig. Gen. Edward Lansdale, Chief of Operations. The Cuba Project. Program Review. January 18, 1962.

Then they listed an initial 32 tasks, to which they later added the spraying of cane fields with a chemical agent aimed at affecting the health of sugar workers. They also included updating the agent system in Cuba, the organization of a "popular movement," infiltration of thousands of spies and weapons of war into the country, and other activities ranging from carrying out psychological warfare campaigns to the drawing up of military contingency plans for an invasion of the island once the conditions were ripe.

The following day, January 19, a meeting was held in Robert Kennedy's offices to analyze the project. Fragments of the notes taken by George McManus, executive assistant to Richard Helms, at that time the CIA deputy director for plans, give an idea of what was discussed there:

> Conclusion Overthrow of Castro is Possible . . . a solution to the Cuban problem today carried top priority in U.S. Govt. No time, money, effort or manpower is to be spared. . . Yesterday. . . the President had indicated to him [Robert Kennedy] that the final chapter had not been written — it's got to be done and will be done. [57]

The Special Group analyzed Lansdale's proposals and sent them to the agencies involved for them to add their opinions. In truth, as life would demonstrate, each of them had taken on the war against Cuba as a personal crusade, and the responses received were so brutal that Lansdale had to revise his plans several times.

In late January 1962, in compliance with an order given by the United States, Cuba was expelled from the Organization of American States (OAS) at a meeting of foreign ministers in Punta del Este, Uruguay; and on February 3, President Kennedy announced a trade embargo against Cuba. On February 20, presidential adviser Walter Rostow asked the members of the North Atlantic Treaty Organization (NATO) to take into

---

[57] *Alleged assassination plots*, 141.

account the decisions of the OAS when they formulated their policies in relation to Cuba. He asked the allies to voluntarily prohibit trade in strategic materials with Cuba and to reduce commerce in general with that country.

In the months of February and March, the Special Group (Augmented) reviewed various proposals for Mongoose. Discussions were based on the 33 tasks condensed into a new document presented by General Lansdale, entitled "The Cuba Project," which proposed seven specific plans and a six-stage timetable for overthrowing the Cuban revolution between March and October 1962.

The plans revolved around actions based inside Cuba and designed to organize the counterrevolution on the island and subordinate it to the "responsible opposition" created in exile; economic, political and psychological warfare projects; military contingency plans; as well as sabotage and intelligence activities designed to promote terror and internal destabilization in order to create the best conditions for the planned aggression. They called for undermining the Cuban government in only eight months. The timetable established was the following:

Phase I: **Action** March 1962. Start moving in.

Phase II: **Build-up** April-July 1962. Activating the necessary operations inside Cuba for revolution and concurrently applying the vital political, economic and military-type support from outside Cuba.

Phase III: **Readiness** 1 August 1962. Check for final policy decision.

Phase IV: **Resistance** August-September 1962. Move into guerrilla operations.

Phase V: **Revolt** First two weeks of October 1962. Open revolt and overthrow of the Communist regime.

Phase VI: **Final** During month of October 1962. Establishment of new government. [58]

---

[58] Brig. Gen. Edward Lansdale, The Cuba Project, February 20, 1962.

After several work sessions the Special Group (Augmented) presented a policy document for the consideration of President Kennedy, which was approved on March 16. It presented the rationale behind the "holy war" which the United States government had declared against Cuba. Part of it reads:

a. In undertaking to cause the overthrow of the target government, the U.S. will make maximum use of indigenous resources, internal and external, but recognizes that final success will require decisive U.S. military intervention.

b. Such indigenous resources as are developed will be used to prepare for and justify this intervention, and thereafter to facilitate and support it. [59]

In the month of April 1962, various crucial events took place. The head of the so-called Cuban Revolutionary Council, José Miró Cardona, met with President Kennedy in the White House. After the meeting Miró Cardona declared that Castro's days were numbered. At the same time William Harvey, head of the CIA's "executive action" group, was reactivating the plans with the Mafia and Tony Varona to assassinate Fidel Castro.

On April 19, the U.S. Armed Forces began military maneuvers on the east coast, from Norfolk, Virginia to Charleston, South Carolina. The exercise was named "Quick Kick," and 83 warships, 300 combat planes and more than 40,000 troops participated in it.

That same month, William Harvey personally saw off several spy teams that left Florida for the island to prepare the conditions to unify the counterrevolutionary organizations there, train the bandits, organize an efficient system of communications with the CIA base and receive hundreds of tons of arms and explosives for the planned popular uprising. Meanwhile, in the United States, all the Cubans who had immigrated since 1959 were questioned exhaustively to uncover any useful information about the

---

[59] Guidelines for Operation Mongoose, March 14, 1962.

situation on the island and, eventually, to discover revolutionary intelligence agents.

According to Operation Mongoose documents declassified in 1988, the CIA reported that "rumors during June of a possible uprising inside Cuba led to further planning for a contingency where a non-U.S. inspired revolt might start inside Cuba . . . ."[60] After hearing this information the Special Group (Augmented) advised the Pentagon to be prepared for such an eventuality. Consequently, General Lansdale gave instructions to General Benjamin Harris, representing the Defense Department, to create a contingency plan. Some of the key aspects of Harris' plan which was circulated at the end of July 1962 were the following:

The United States will support and sustain the rebellion in Cuba through all its resources, including the use of U.S. military force to assure replacement of the Communist regime with a new Cuban government acceptable to the United States . . . .

The initial stages of a spontaneous revolt will be supported by the United States through propaganda, covert operations, and other actions as necessary [rest of sentence blacked out]. In the event that the revolt spreads as a popular movement against the Communist regime, the United States should be capable of rapid military action to forestall a concerted and drastic reprisal program in the interest of humanity and the mission of this plan. . . . [61]

On July 25, in a report to the Special Group (Augmented) in which the results of the Operation Mongoose plans were analyzed, General Lansdale explained the progress made in political, economic and psychological actions, as well as the military preparations for a decisive "United States defensive capacity in the face of a military invasion."

---

[60] Brig. Gen. Edward Lansdale, The Cuba Project, February 20, 1962.

[61] Lansdale, *Memorandum. Subject: United States Contingency Plan No. 2. Cuba.* Partially declassified and released on January 5, 1989 by the National Security Council.

It also referred to certain CIA accomplishments, such as the infiltration of 11 groups of agents into the island, one of which had organized a structure of 250 men in Pinar del Río Province. In spite of setbacks, the intelligence gathering activities were rated as "superior," as was the sabotage that had been damaging the Cuban economy and the Pentagon's plan which had "successfully established a capacity for military action against Cuba."

The pressing issue, declared Lansdale, was to develop plans and objectives for the next phase of Mongoose. He proposed four possible alternatives in the following stages, incorporating the suggestions of the different agencies represented in the Special Group:

a. Cancel operational plans; treat Cuba as a [Communist] Bloc nation; protect Hemisphere from it, or

b. Exert all possible diplomatic, economic, psychological and other pressures to overthrow the Castro-Communist regime without overt employment of U.S. military, or

c. Commit U.S. to help Cubans overthrow the Castro-Communist regime, with a step-by-step phasing to ensure success, including the use of U.S. military force if required at the end, or

d. Use a provocation and overthrow the Castro-Communist regime by U.S. military force. [62]

After a number of discussions inside the Special Group (Augmented) and with the approval of President Kennedy, "Plan B plus" was selected and presented as Memorandum No. 181, signed on August 23 by McGeorge Bundy, as directed by the U.S. President. [63]

A new euphemism was thereby slipped into the official language. The option was approved which called for no direct military intervention, but the appellation "plus" was tacked on for the purpose of including it should the circumstances so

---

[62] Brig. Gen. Edward Lansdale, The Cuba Project, February 20, 1962.

[63] Brig. Gen. Edward Lansdale, The Cuba Project, February 20, 1962.

warrant. After all, the military plans were already in place and all that was lacking was for the proper conditions to be created so that President Kennedy could give his authorization. However, some prominent figures in the U.S. government at the time still insist that was never the intention. However, taking into account the history of the relations between Cuba and the United States, who could doubt that such an order would be given as the result of a provocation staged by them against their own Naval Base at Guantánamo, for example, or the bombing of a U.S. ship, as occurred a century ago with the *Maine*?

One of the most sophisticated projects of the U.S. administration was its venture into the field of psychological warfare, under the responsibility of the United States Information Agency (USIA), the mechanism created to spread the American way of life and whose mission it was to "brainwash" the Cubans. Psychological warfare has been and continues to be one of the most diabolical weapons that the United States has employed frequently against the Cuban revolution for more than 30 years. Its basic objective has been to demoralize the people in order to then oust the established government from the island.

U.S. documents from as early as 1951 offered the first definitions of this type of warfare. The military dictionary of the U.S. Armed Forces had explained psychological warfare as actions taken on the part of one or several nations in propaganda and other information media against enemy groups, neutrals or friends in order to influence their beliefs, sentiments, opinions and/or conduct in favor of the policies and objectives of the nation or group of nations which this would serve.

In other words, its purpose is to undermine, destabilize and overthrow the government of the country against which it is employed. John Foster Dulles, Secretary of State under President Dwight D. Eisenhower and one of the architects of the secret war against Cuba, referring to the importance of this method, lamented having spent millions of dollars preparing for a war with weapons, but very few for a war of ideas.

In the same era, the director of the USIA noted that the simple introduction of doubt in the minds of the people is in itself a great success. For these reasons, psychological warfare was crucial to the Operation Mongoose arsenal. The Cuba Project included a whole section dedicated to this purpose. There, several of the USIA's goals in this respect were defined, including:

> First create a sympathetic climate and motivate the forces for the liberation of Cuba; second [blacked out]; third, demonstrate concern for the situation of the [Cuban] refugees, particularly orphaned children; fourth, demonstrate the failure of the Cuban regime to comply with the promises made by the July 26 Movement; fifth, accentuate the intolerable conditions in Cuba and the situation of the Cubans on the island; sixth, [blacked out]; seventh, publish that common citizens, not just the rich, have fled from Cuba.
>
> Considerations: all of the mass media should be utilized for spiritual resources (such as the Prayer for Cuba by Bishop Boza Masvidal, who has a genuine revolutionary background). Reclaim the ideas of Martí, making use of his memory to emphasize the distancing from the communists. Popularize songs which allude to these slogans. . . . Mrs. Kennedy would be particularly effective in the visits to refugee children (in one camp near Miami there are around a thousand children who left Cuba without their parents). The impact caused by the recent visits by the presidents of Venezuela and Colombia to these camps suggests this. Disseminate throughout the continent articles, documentaries, cartoons, etc. which denigrate the Cuban regime.
>
> Elaborate information with statistics about the refugees who continually arrive in the United States, Jamaica, Mexico, Venezuela and Spain for the propaganda campaigns against the Castro regime. . . .

In mid-1962, more than 10 anti-Cuba radio stations were transmitting programs specializing in news, music, religion and other subjects. Through them orders were systematically given to carry out sabotage and terrorist acts and to spread false rumors, so that in effect they took on an espionage function.

Another of the objectives of this war was to discredit the Cuban leaders, Fidel Castro in particular. As if attempting to kill him physically wasn't enough, they also tried to assassinate him morally.

In a document dated August 7, 1962, Donald M. Wilson, the United States Information Agency representative for Operation Mongoose, mentioned the results of some of the USIA work against Cuba and planned for the final offensive which, deceived by its own lies, the group was convinced was near:

> Where other access is denied us, radio is the best means to reach the Cuban people. It is USIA's view that our short wave capability (VOA) is operating at the most efficient technical level, with nine hours of broadcasting a day in Spanish. Three of the nine hours are devoted specifically to Cuba. . . .
>
> The establishment of a medium wave capability would be desirable. It is indeed possible to broadcast a strong signal into Cuba, and USIA had made a study of 10 possible sites to locate transmitters. . . .

With regard to improving information capability throughout Latin America, the document continued:

> Our capability will depend on the availability of funds. The Latin American program was stepped-up 32 percent in fiscal year 1962, and it will be stepped-up 26 percent more in fiscal year 1963, so the availability of even more funds is a real problem.
>
> Here are examples of current programming which could be augmented:
>
> 1. *Radio:* We could step-up our production of packaged radio programs for placement on radio stations throughout Latin America.

2. *Cartoon Books*: The Agency has done six anti-Castro cartoon books (5 million copies), having a widespread impact over the area. This program could be stepped-up.
3. *Motion Pictures:* The Agency has produced an animated film on Cuban land reform theme and has two more films in the pipeline. An increased production of films, although expensive, could be instituted. [64]

In a September 11 memorandum to General Lansdale, Wilson elaborated:

In December 1962 the VOA's new Greenville, North Carolina facility will become operational giving a substantial increase in signal strength.

Programming is built around hard news and commentary, features and local Cuban happenings, particularly items not carried in the Castro/Communist media.

With regard to medium wave transmission, he noted that:

Radio Americas, operated under a cover company, is a directly controlled radio station broadcasting on 1160 KC (also short wave) with a power of 50 kilowatts. The station broadcasts ten and one half hours daily, seven days a week, from Swan Island in the Caribbean. Programs are written and taped by Cuban exiles working under Agency supervision and control.

The programs are directed to a general audience, with special emphasis on farm and labor groups. Up-to-the-minute news programs are broadcast live on an hourly basis and taped editorials deal with current political problems. The

---

[64] Donald M. Wilson, quoted in The Cuba Project, August 7, 1962, Partially declassified and released on January 5, 1989 by the National Security Council.

station offers a broad range of music and entertainment, [and] provides a daily religious program. . . .

Three commercial stations carry anti-Castro programs purchased by a front organization which is controlled directly by the Agency. . . .

CIA has the capability for intruding on the dormant audio channels of Havana TV, utilizing small vessels. . . .

Stratovision (beaming a TV signal from an airplane in flight) offers definite possibilities for short-term purely tactical utilization of TV. Preliminary studies indicate that air-borne TV transmitters operating over U.S. territory and territorial waters could beam a strong signal into the Havana area, using presently vacant channels. Our estimates indicate that it would probably take the Cubans from 15 to 21 days to engineer and put into operation an effective jamming system. This operation would cost approximately $250,000, assuming that aircraft and crews would be made available by DOD [Department of Defense] and programm-ing and technical staff would come from USIA.[65]

Once again they miscalculated. The subversive TV signal which has long formed part of the U.S. war against Cuba, did not last even one minute on the air when they finally tried to set it up in 1990.

---

[65] Donald M. Wilson, Memorandum for Brig. Gen. Edward G. Lansdale, September 11, 1962.

CHAPTER 8

The conspirators

The final months of 1961 were characterized by a decline in counterrevolutionary activity. The counterrevolution was discouraged by the blows which had been delivered and the vigilance and the enthusiasm with which the people devoted themselves to building the new society. At the end of 1961 the Directorate of Intelligence of the CIA assessed the Cuban situation and noted the state of decomposition of the counter-revolutionary groups and organizations and a decrease in expectations for a rapid invasion by the U.S. armed forces. Among the final recommendations of the document was that some action should be taken soon in order to revive falling spirits. It also suggested another injection of weapons and other resources to help get the now unreliable counterrevolutionary bands back into action.

A study of the Cuban scene led them to the false belief that the most favorable territories for the uprising should meet certain criteria: for example, intricate mountain ranges which could harbor a strong and well-supplied guerrilla nucleus, distant from urban centers, scarce means of communication, and a rural population sufficiently backward culturally and politically to be easily susceptible to indoctrination by agents.

The major metropolitan centers were not forgotten, but the paranoia caused by the blows dealt to the counterrevolution by Cuban State Security, and the spirit with which the workers supported the revolutionary process, led them to relegate the importance of work in the cities and soon erase them from their organizational plans, considering them only as targets for large-scale terrorism. Out of these proposals grew the theory that a select group of men, artificially placed in a given favorable social environment would be capable of causing a popular revolt and spreading the uprising throughout the country. An army of terrorists was contracted and hundreds of them began to train in military skills, clandestine operations, intelligence, psychological warfare and communications, in order to later infiltrate the country through preselected areas. Once inside, they would proceed to recruit the "uncultured and unpoliticized," and set up communications, supplies, and routes to exfiltrate selected cadres and pave the way for the decisive offensive.

One of the CIA's priorities was the reorganization of the internal front. The counterrevolutionary groups and bands were structures that already existed and should be used. For that reason, political action teams of agents were organized and given the mission of assessing the state of these organizations and then restructuring them with rigid compartmentalization measures, so that they could later be armed and sent into battle. William Harvey met with several of these agents during the early days of 1962, to personally instruct them in the tasks they were to carry out. These included Manuel Guillot Castellanos, Julio Hernández Rojo, Esteban Márquez Novo, Félix Rodríguez, Eugenio Martínez, Clemente Inclán Werner, Luis Fernández Rocha, Miguel and Ramón Orozco, Alberto del Busto, Pedro Cameron and Manuel del Valle.

Each person at the meeting had a mission. Guillot, Márquez Novo, Fernández Rocha, Cameron and del Valle would be infiltrated into Cuba to reorganize the counterrevolution, while the rest would take charge of marine supply. Of all of them, the greatest hope was placed in Guillot Castellanos. His experience in the MRR, where he worked alongside Manuel Artime, had earned him the reputation as an excellent organizer. He came from a Catholic background, had been a militant member of the University Association, and had joined the counterrevolutionary struggle back in 1959. By the time he was recruited by the CIA, he already had broad undercover experience in Cuba and had the support of the internal and external leaders of the organization. His friendship with Juan Falcón Zammar, alias Esteban, the coordinator of the MRR on the island, guaranteed him a position of influence in that structure, which was the CIA's favorite instrument for the Mongoose projects.

The strategy that he pursued was to unite the principal counterrevolutionary groups. Several dozen of them still existed, but not all of them were trusted by the Agency which knew that the G-2 had learned hard lessons in the early years, and presumed that by now Cuban Security had penetrated some of the groups.

Guillot was to select those that could be trusted in order to give them preference in the plans: their national chiefs would be brought to the United States and their provincial structures compartmentalized, making their communications and supply systems independent of those in other areas. In short, local organizations were being created that would be difficult for the Cuban authorities to discover.

No time was wasted. The resources began to arrive. The flow was not as steady as desired, but it was sufficient to carry out the campaign of sabotage and terrorism. From January to August 1962, a total of 5,780 counterrevolutionary actions were recorded, of which 718 were acts of sabotage of economically important targets. The offensive included the destruction of millions of arrobas of sugarcane and warehouses of other merchandise through arson, the murder of revolutionaries, attacks on merchant vessels, bombings of coastal hotels — in short, an all-out war.

Among the most active organizations were the Christian Democratic Movement, People's Revolutionary Movement, Movement for the Recovery of the Revolution, Revolutionary Unity, Anticommunist Armed Forces, Rescate, Montecristi, Revolutionary Action, Martí Democratic Movement, November 30 Movement, Triple A, Democratic Insurrectional Movement, National Liberation Army, Revolutionary Directorate, Anticommunist Organizations Bloc, Second National Front of the

Escambray, and the Revolutionary Insurrectional Anticommunist Front.

On January 14, Guillot entered Havana Province through a point on the north coast known as Roca, near Santa Cruz del Norte. Within a few days he began to establish contacts with the counterrevolutionary leaders, including Falcón Zammar. With great effort, he was able to stop the exodus of the cadres into exile. He had many meetings and conferences and then on March 5, slipped back out of the country and returned to the United States. He carried in his briefcase proposals and plans in line with the orientation given him by the CIA.

In Miami, William Harvey met with him and described the operation in detail. They chose five organizations to make up the so-called Unity Front, and after reviewing the details of the operation, on May 1 Guillot returned to Cuba through the same point on the coast.

In the meantime, the Cuban State Security Department did not remain inactive. It had been hitting the counterrevolutionary structures and had captured their main leaders. It was fully aware of the importance of the CIA plan, and began a tenacious pursuit of the infiltrated agents. On May 8, Falcón Zammar and other MRR leaders were picked up; and on May 29, Guillot himself was captured while waiting for his contacts to help him flee the country. Some passages of the declarations made by the detainees in the legal offices of Cuban State Security reveal part of the Mongoose plans, and above all, reflect the mood of the counterrevolution. As Juan Falcón Zammar testified:

In the final days of December 1961, or in early January [1962], the replacement for Lucas, the coordinator of Las Villas Province, was in Havana. In those days we were already in the process of dissolving the movement and we had begun a total recess of all activities.

I would like to explain the reasons why we had decided to make these decisions about the dissolution of the movement. In the first place, there was the ideological reason. Until that moment we had preserved the illusion that we alone, or with little help from the United States, were capable of toppling the communist government of Cuba. We thought that the Americans would give us disinterested aid, aid for which they would ask nothing in return. Therefore we had arrived at the decision to disband the movement, because we knew that the Americans were not going to help us disinterestedly. . . .

Another element that led us to this conclusion was that we offered them dozens of points on the coast where they could supply us with materials and resources. Then they started the same old story. The Yankees are not interested in solving the problem of Cuba. The only thing they want is for us to commit sabotage and more sabotage, place bombs, create fear, and carry out terrorist plans, so that agitation will engulf the country and the government will have to carry out a violent repression with much bloodshed which they can then use in their propaganda throughout Latin America. They can tell the world of the horrors of communism in Cuba. . . .

All this caused us to lose our faith in the struggle and disillusionment spread through the ranks of the activists of the MRR.

A total recess of all activities was declared and everyone was told to avoid meetings. Therefore, many began to make plans to leave the country or to return to their homes if they believed that was still possible.

In the month of January, Manuel Guillot, alias Rogelio, infiltrated the country and assured us that now we would be supplied with arms, that the Americans would be disposed to help us and that they wanted to resolve the problem of Cuba as soon as possible; that the Americans were only waiting for the internal problems of the organization to be resolved and for us to give them points on the coast for infiltration.

In mid-February, we reorganized the structures of the movement. The plan which was conceived was to prepare one or two great acts of sabotage and one or two important assassination attempts. . . .

Rogelio brought a plan for reorganizing the movement on the basis of a strict compartmentalization, and that month we began the work . . . .

In mid-March, we prepared an assassination attempt on Dr. Juan Marinello at the University of Havana, but at the last minute "someone" stole the car we had planned to use and everything fell apart.

At the end of the same month Rogelio left the country, taking with him the man in charge of contacts with the guerrillas, Arturo Mugarra Pupo.

On May 1, Rogelio infiltrated again, through the coast at Club Náutico. The following day he explained to me the plans he brought for uniting the groups which he considered the five most important organizations: the MRP, MDC, November 30, DRE and MRR.

This unity was based on the military aspect. We national coordinators were to form an advisory board which would be based outside of Cuba, in a U.S. city other than Miami. [66]

For his part, Manuel Guillot Castellanos described in detail all of the activity deployed, in particular of the months following his secret reentry into the country:

Upon my return from the United States in January 1962, I began to restructure the MRR for security reasons, closing down various secretariats in the provinces, such as provincial, civilian and military coordinators, and the security and finance secretariats. These positions would only exist on a regional level, since a G-2 penetration of these positions would allow them to control the structure at this level.

I had known Arturo Mugarra for a long time, so I named him national secretary of rebellion because he was already in contact with the guerrillas. I also met the head of

---

[66] Declarations by Juan Falcón Zammar to Cuban State Security. May 1962.

the rebels, Congo Pacheco, through Arturo. . . . Troadio, the coordinator of the movement in Matanzas, who also arranged an interview with Pichi Catalá, the chief of the rebels in that province. . . .

An attempt was prepared for March 13 against Juan Marinello in the University of Havana, but it failed when the car we planned to use was stolen that very day. . . .

I was in contact with DRE leaders Roberto Quintairos and Hans Gengler Ebner, and we also met with José Prince, alias Neno, the MRP's national coordinator, who told us he had already talked with the coordinators of the MDC, November 30, Rescate and Unidad, to get them to join us. I explained that I needed to consult with people outside the country, and that I would soon be traveling to Florida to explain the plans, and we left it that we would firm things up when I returned. . . .

I appointed Alberto Sowers head of intelligence, but he was practically unable to carry out that work because of lack of preparation, so we had the idea of sending him to the United States for training. . . .

On March 29 we slipped out of the country with Arturo Mugarra, Congo Pacheco's nephew, and one of Pichí Catalá's assistants, who were to be trained in guerrilla warfare in the Florida camps. . . . A raft came to take us out to the reefs. The boat was medium-sized and had a Cuban crew we didn't know. We reached the American coast the next day, and a motor boat picked us up and took us to a place where there were three automobiles waiting for us. My companions got into two of the cars, and I rode in the other one with Tomás, the CIA official.

In the safe house where I was taken, an American known as Larry went over the secret writing with me, as well as covert techniques and the use of key words on the radio. Tomás gave me a tape recorder so that in my spare time I could record all the movements and interviews that I made in Cuba. I also brought up the subject of uniting the organizations that I had talked about with Prince, the MRP coordinator.

After consulting, Tomás authorized the formation of the bloc, but he emphasized the need for compartment-alization in order to avoid penetration by the G-2. He told me that after the Unity was set up, I was to take the heads of the five movements outside of the country for a meeting where they would be briefed about the plans they were to carry out. . . .

At dawn on May 1, a raft deposited us on the coast of Santa Cruz del Norte.

On the second of May, I met with Juan Falcón, alias Esteban. . . I explained to him the instructions regarding the union of the five organizations. The following day, we met with the coordinators of the MDC, MRP and November 30 in the car belonging to Quintairos, the DRE coordinator. There I explained the plans to them informally, and we set a meeting for the following Sunday in Varadero in Matanzas. Unfortunately, Quintairos was arrested the following week and the meeting was held without the presence of the DRE. We set up a new meeting, but that week Esteban and several MRR cadres were arrested, among them Manuel Reyes, the radio operator, so we lost contact with the outside and those who were training in Miami couldn't return. . . . [67]

During the first quarter of 1962, an important meeting took place between the heads of the bandits who operated in the mountain stronghold of the Escambray. The place selected was the area known as Las Llanadas de Gómez, in the most dense part of the sierra. Gathered there were Tomás San Gil, Julio Emilio Carretero, Nilo Armando Florencia, Congo Pacheco, Jesús Mollinedo, Alberto Martínez Andrade, Benito Campos, Floro Camacho and others. The topic of discussion was the selection of

---

[67] Declarations by Juan Manuel Guillot Castellanos to Cuban State Security. June 1962.

the head of the "National Liberation Army," which the CIA required to unify the activities and organize the supplies.

Tomás San Gil was elected. His qualifications included broad experience as an assassin of peasants and literacy teachers. Besides, the CIA supported him, and in the meeting between the agent Guillot Castellanos and various bandit chiefs this had been one of the conditions imposed for obtaining recognition and assistance.

At that time there existed in Las Villas Province 41 bands containing approximately 500 men. More than 30 additional groups, amounting to several hundred men, operated in other parts of the country, to which could be added the collaboration of many peasants and agricultural workers intimidated by their former landlords turned counterrevolutionary leaders.

From the U.S. Naval Base at Guantánamo, the CIA prepared to organize a front of bandits in the eastern mountains to supplement the disturbances that were projected for that year. Several agents had been trained to penetrate the southern part of the Sierra Maestra and the mountain strongholds of Baracoa, Sagua de Tánamo and Yateras. They included Amancio Mosqueda, Emilio Vera, Tico Herrera, José Rodríguez Peña, Alcibiades Macías, Pablo Pupo Cruz and others. In the CIA's base of operations in Miami it was hoped that these bandit fronts would be ready to function sometime between May and June. Their main objectives were to spread terror, destabilize society and destroy agricultural production — particularly sugarcane — in order to paralyze the national economy. Nevertheless, the revolution wasted no time in responding; thousands of combatants were mobilized in the struggle against the bandits. Some were quickly captured, and others killed. Furthermore, dozens of tons of military supplies dropped by parachute from planes proceeding from the United States fell into the hands of the Rebel Army.

Between January and March 1962, 150 counter-revolutionaries were killed and several hundred more were captured in 98 battles in the Escambray. In June, the State Security forces had concluded an operation against the National Democratic Front (FND), which was composed of 20 organizations. The main officials of the organization had been military officers during the Batista dictatorship.

By the middle of the year the bands were on the defensive, hiding in caves and dense thickets, waiting once again for the United States to pull the chestnuts from the fire. In the Sierra de los Organos in Pinar del Río Province, on July 22, the bandit chieftain Pastor Rodríguez Roda, alias Cara Linda [Pretty Face], was killed in combat with the security forces. A fugitive since 1959 when he murdered several young revolutionaries, "Pretty Face" was known for his cruel repression of the peasants of the region. Weeks later, on August 23, Filiberto Coto Gómez, alias El Pipero [the Piper], who operated in the southern part of Havana Province, was also captured. He had murdered dozens of agricultural workers, torched thousands of arrobas of sugarcane, and shot up various locations. He had a network of collaborators composed of 106 wealthy farmers from the countryside, all of whom were also arrested.

The first half of 1962 ended with the absolute failure of the efforts of the Mongoose forces to organize a clandestine army in the mountains of Cuba. Meanwhile, the energy of Mongoose was being focused on the plan for an internal uprising that various counter-revolutionary groups, led by the Anticommunist Liberation Forces, were trying to organize. The CIA had learned of these groups through the subversive activities they had carried out in various localities. By July, the counterrevolutionaries had worked out the details of the insurrection and began to coordinate them with their leaders in exile.

One of the CIA agents among the conspirators was Bernardo Alvarez Perdomo, national coordinator of Revolutionary Unity, who sent frequent reports about the sedition. The plan was to organize one hundred commandos who would take various strategic locations in the nation's capital. They would also dynamite the electrical plants that served the city and other vital objectives. The weapons taken from the military quarters — so the conspirators assumed — would be turned over to groups of counter-revolutionary activists who would then join the fray.

Under these circumstances, the United States would have to intervene and bring down the Cuban revolution.

The FAL was also given the task of forming a task force to assassinate the principal leaders of the revolution in their homes. The date selected was August 30, and Perdomo communicated this to the CIA through a European embassy.

There were conflicts among the counterrevolutionary leaders. Some thought that the proper conditions had not been prepared, but no one could persuade the FAL to wait a little longer. Thus, when the State Security Department learned of the plans on August 29, they decided to take immediate action, and they arrested the main conspirators and confiscated their weapons and other military equipment. During the judicial proceedings that followed, several of the counterrevolutionaries admitted their goals. Pedro Manuel Silio Matos testified:

> In July I was named military coordinator of the municipality of Marianao. A few days later I was promoted to head of operations for Havana Province. At that time they explained the plans and supplied me with various contacts in the Navy and the police.
>
> During the following weeks, I studied the objectives that were to be attacked, including the Tallapiedra electrical plant, the headquarters of the Revolutionary Armed Forces, the airport, the [Naval] Academy in Mariel and the radio and television retransmitters.[68]

Bernabé Corominas Portuondo disclosed:

> I was in charge of contacting the CIA at the Guantánamo Naval Base. We drew up the plans for the area bordering the base where the weapons were to have been delivered.[69]

---

[68] Declarations by Pedro Manuel Silio Matos to Cuban State Security. September 1962.
[69] Declarations by Bernabé Corominas to Cuban State Security. October 1962.

Another detainee, Ventura Suárez Díaz, alias Joseíto, declared:

> I organized nine commandos in the city of Havana for the purpose of capturing the police stations in the capital. I was also in contact with those in charge of the movement in the provinces of Las Villas, Camagüey and Oriente to specify the tasks that each group was to carry out on August 30. The arms were hidden in previously selected safe houses. . . . The coordinators of Revolutionary Unity, November 30 Movement, and the DRE had told me that they agreed to participate in the uprising. . . . [70]

The final element of proof that the CIA knew about, directed, and participated in these plans was a cable later declassified by the U.S. government, referring to this subversive project, which read:

> Possible counterrevolutionary uprisings in Cuba at the end of August.
> Date distr. 28 August 1962
>
> Precedence routine
> 1. The Unidad Revolucionaria (UR) has sent a representative to brief the UR in exile regarding a plan for an uprising to take place in Cuba in August. Also, an officer of the UR in Cuba met with the second national coordinator of the Frente Anti-comunista de Liberacion (FAL) to discuss this plan. According to all indications, this plan will be carried out before 30 August.
>
> 2. This planned action will be suicidal for those who carry it out, but the UR in Cuba is certain that if this plan is initiated, the UR members will have no choice but to participate with whatever means at their disposal. The UR is being put into a position of having to participate in the

---

[70] Declarations by Ventura Suárez to Cuban State Security. September 1962.

action because it has been privy to the discussions held
regarding this plan.

3. It is certain that the Cuban regime will use this action as
justification to try to eliminate all clandestine resistance in
Cuba. Government authorities will search the homes of
resistance members; under these circumstances, in the
opinion of the UR members, it would be better to die
fighting.

4. The UR in Cuba has sent an urgent appeal for men and
equipment to its members in exile. The UR in Cuba has
warned the exile members that should the government of
Cuba decide that the entry of men and equipment into Cuba
has the semblance of an invasion, it will then turn its forces
against the "invaders," and not against the
counterrevolutionary forces within Cuba.

5.   [blacked out. Not declassified.]

6.   [blacked out. Not declassified.]

7.   Field dissem: CINCARIB, CINCLANT [71]

At that time, the enemies of the revolution had decided to do
everything in their power to win the confidence of their masters,
and in spite of the blows they had received from the security
forces and the people who kept vigilance in the countryside and
the cities, they struggled hard to achieve their ends.

In the following days, the internal front was again
restructured, changing its name, and thus the Anticommunist
Civic Resistance (RCA) was born, made up of a dozen groups.
Documents from its founding meeting testify to its purposes:

Somewhere in Havana at 4:00 p.m. on September 3, 1962,
the undersigned, representatives of various organizations and

---

[71] Declassified CIA cable referring to Operation Mongoose.

groups in the underground struggle, agree to form the National Resistance Board to guide and direct the internal struggle, which will end in the defeat of the communist forces which today imprison our beloved country. [72]

It was yet another subversive plan operating with the complicity of the Naval Intelligence Service from the Guantánamo Naval Base and the CIA. Through agent Ricardo Lorié, more than 250 weapons of all types had been introduced into the country from the Naval Base for the purpose of reorganizing and rearming the internal counterrevolution. The plan once again consisted of a provocation of their own naval base, utilizing a commando unit of 150 men who had been trained at the top secret CIA base near New Orleans in the United States. At the same time the RCA organizations were to attack key points in the country, such as military bases and other strategic and economic targets, and an attempt was to be made on the life of Fidel Castro.

Luis David Rodríguez González, was one of the primary conspirators, together with Ricardo Olmedo Moreno, Luis Rodríguez and others. They maintained close ties with Tony Varona, who had supplied the men for the commando unit from Miami with the collaboration of the omnipresent Mafia, and who was following the murderous project closely.

An unexpected development for the United States — the installation of Soviet missiles in Cuba in the fall of 1962 — dramatically interrupted the plans for a military aggression. The history of this crisis is well known. The world came to the brink of a nuclear holocaust and all corners of the world could see the genocide that the United States was trying to commit against the people of Cuba.

A few years ago, the U.S. government began to publish some of the documents by the official agencies concerning Operation Mongoose. Perhaps, the main documents will never be made

---

[72] Report from the Cuban State Security Department on the founding of the Resisitencia Cívica Anticomunista (Anticommunist Civic Resistance). September 1962.

public; however sufficient evidence appears in those that have been released to expose the malicious intentions of imperialism toward the island.

The events initiated by the October Missile Crisis persuaded the conspirators that a Yankee military invasion was inevitable, and they decided to postpone their plans and hide in safe places not foreseeing that, just like the Bay of Pigs, the revolutionary forces would take care of the *gusanos*.

CHAPTER 9

Executive Action

During the year 1962 and within the context of Operation Mongoose, the CIA and the counterrevolutionary organizations dreamed up dozens of plans to assassinate Fidel Castro. It was the moment when the United States administration was most determined to rid itself of the Cuban government believing that decapitating the revolution was fundamental to achieving its objectives. At the same time, Cuba found it's voice muffled by the international media monopolies while being the subject of a vicious worldwide disinformation campaign.

It wouldn't be until several years later, after the Watergate scandal and the declarations made in a U.S. court by the mafioso John Rosselli, that the U.S. Senate investigated the plans from the 1960s for eliminating foreign political leaders hostile to the policies of Washington, including Fidel Castro.

But it is clear that not all of the criminal projects carried out with the approval of and directed by the U.S. authorities were revealed. The most secret and most compromising documents are still guarded in security boxes and buried in the depths of the Washington bureaucracy. However, the central archives of the Cuban State Security Department also have ample evidence and documented proof of these deeds.

One irrefutable example of the numerous assassination plots against Fidel Castro during 1962 was presented in a U.S. Senate investigation. The Senate report states that both Bissell and

Harvey remembered a meeting in November 1961, in which the latter was instructed to take charge of contacting John Rosselli as part of the ZR/RIFLE project. Harvey's notes placed the meeting on November 15, during the period in which he was relieved of other responsibilities in order to take over as head of Task Force W, which directed the CIA activities against Cuba.[73]

The 1967 report by the Inspector General of the CIA which investigated these acts established that, "After Harvey took over the Castro operation he ran it as one aspect of ZRRIFLE [sic]. . . In addition, Bissell's instructions to Harvey on November 15, 1961, preceded by five months the reactivation of the assassination operation by the CIA and the Mafia against Fidel Castro. . . ."[74]

According to the 1975 U.S. Senate investigation into the CIA's plans to assassinate foreign political leaders, in early April 1962 William Harvey — who testified that he was acting on explicit orders from the new deputy director of the CIA, Richard Helms — asked Colonel Sheffield Edwards, chief of security for the Agency, to put him in contact with Rosselli. Through his subordinate James O'Connell, he went to the Mafia chief who explained that it was possible to use Cuban collaborators to take out a contract on Fidel Castro. O'Connell recalls that in the beginning Rosselli did not trust Harvey, but later they developed a close friendship.[75]

On April 8 and 9, 1962, Harvey, Rosselli and O'Connell met again in New York. A note in the files of the CIA laboratories indicates that some poison capsules were turned over to O'Connell on April 18, 1962. Days later, on the 25th of that month, Harvey and Rosselli met in Miami, with the former being aware that the mafioso had reestablished contact with the same Cuban who had participated in an earlier operation on the eve of the Bay of Pigs. Harvey gave the capsules to Rosselli, explaining that they "would work anywhere and at any time with

---

[73] *Memorandum for the record*, 38-39.

[74] *Memorandum for the record*, 40.

[75] *Alleged assassination plots*, 82-85.

anything,"[76] and Rosselli responded that the Cubans intended to use them to assassinate Che Guevara, Raúl Castro and Fidel Castro. Harvey agreed, authorizing them to select their own targets.

The Cuban assassin had requested weapons and communications equipment to carry out the operation, which were supplied from the warehouses of the CIA operational base in Miami. Harvey kept abreast of the progress of the operation, learning that in May 1962 the capsules and the weapons had arrived in Cuba. On June 21, Rosselli informed him that the unidentified Cuban had sent a team of three men to the island to supervise the action. Harvey and Rosselli met once again in Miami on September 7 and 11, 1962, where the latter reported that another team was being prepared to penetrate Fidel Castro's bodyguards, and that the poison capsules were still safe. Harvey replied that he had serious doubts that the operation would ever be carried out.

At the beginning of 1963, Harvey paid Rosselli — according to CIA files — $2,700 to cover some of his expenses, putting an end to the operation, and ordering the mafioso to "cool his relations with the Cubans."

The Senate version is, without a doubt, true. It nevertheless lacks certain essential details needed to comprehend the entire scope of the plot. As is now known, the mysterious "Cuban" recruited by the Mafia was Tony Varona, who continued serving as a CIA agent although he was unaware of his central role in the plans that organized crime had sold him on.

Bissell's successor as the Agency's deputy director for covert operations, Richard Helms, was obstinate about not wanting to know who the executioners were that had been selected, reasoning that this would free him from responsibility for the crime.[77] And so history repeated itself: the CIA contracted the

---

[76] *Alleged assassination plots*, 84.

[77] John Ranelagh, *The rise and decline of the CIA*, (London: Sceptre, 1988), 402. Richard Helms was to testify that the post-Bay of Pigs attempts to kill Castro were one of the biggest mistakes of his career. "I have apologized for this," he said to the House Select Committee on

Mafia which planned the assassination with men and resources from the CIA itself. Only this time something even more bizarre was about to occur.

In the early days of 1962, Rescate, Tony Varona's organization in Cuba, was as demoralized as the other groups. At this time, CIA agent Norberto Martínez, who had been infiltrated into the island a few weeks earlier, began to recruit the leaders of Rescate to set up intelligence networks, diverting them from political activities. Varona knew nothing of this, and through a CIA collaborator — the information attaché at the Spanish embassy, Alejandro Vergara Maury — he sent his accomplices a long letter of instructions and the new capsules made in the laboratory of Joseph Scheider, chief of the CIA Technical Services Division.

At the end of April, Vergara summoned to his office in the Spanish embassy in Havana the contact given him by Varona, who turned out to be María Leopoldina Grau Alsina, better known as Polita, the niece of the former president Ramón Grau San Martín. Days later, Polita Grau again went to the Spanish embassy at Vergara's request. There she met with Jaime Capedevilla, attaché and spy, who questioned her about the possibility of carrying out the operation, emphasizing the instructions given by Varona, who had been pressuring him in repeated telephone calls to meet with the conspirators.

Polita met with Alberto Cruz Caso, his brother Ramón, and Manuel de Jesús Campanioni Souza, a former gambler at the casinos in the Sans Souci and the Hotel Havana Libre, and an old friend of the U.S. gangster-turned-patriot Santos Trafficante. She explained the orders from her boss and displayed the capsules.

Assassinations in September 1978. "I can't do any more than apologize on public television that it was an error of judgment on my part. There was great pressure on us at that time to try to find connections in Cuba. For my part in this and to the extent I had anything to do with it, I am heartily sorry. I cannot do any more than apologize." House Select Committee on Assassinations, Investigation of the Assassination of President John F. Kennedy, Vol. IV, 181.

"Our task consists of finding a person who can give the poison to Fidel without arousing suspicion," she explained. "I've been thinking about our connections at the Hotel Havana Libre. Perhaps one of the men from the organization is willing to take on the mission. We all know that Fidel frequents that place, and an opportunity will present itself. . . ."

In that simple manner, Polita Grau outlined the assassination. Campanioni indicated his agreement and accepted the responsibility of finding a suitable executioner.

Days later, Campanioni met with several members of Rescate who worked in the hotel, among them Santos de la Caridad Pérez Nuñez, Bartolomé Pérez García and José Saceiro. The first was a food service worker in the cafeteria, the others maitre d's in the restaurant. They had known each other for years, so it was not difficult for Campanioni to approach his friends. Bartolomé had been the owner of the Bulnes and El Gato Tuerto bars. His resentment stemmed from the fact that the revolution had closed down his brothels. Santos de la Caridad and José Saceiro's motivations were different. Both missed their old bosses and dreamed of their return. The job was one that could win points for them; perhaps when the North Americans took possession of the hotel again, they would reward them with good jobs.

Once he had convinced the three would-be assassins, Campanioni divided the capsules among them, so that each could have them handy when the occasion presented itself. Until that time they had been hidden by Polita in the house of a collaborator, Herminia Suárez Payat, who was happy to be rid of them.

Time passed and Fidel did not come near the trap that had been set for him. At that point another member of the group came up with a new plan. Miguel Matamoros Valle, who had been a pilot in Batista's army, proposed to poison Commander Efigenio Ameijeiras, taking advantage of the fact that he frequented El Recodo Cafeteria on the Malecón and F Street in the center of Vedado. Matamoros assured him the crime would so move the public that there would be a mass demonstration of mourning, which Fidel would certainly attend. At that moment, someone could shoot him and then get lost in the crowd.

The CIA in Miami was consulted by means of a message in secret code. Nobody there knew of the plans agents had made with the Mafia and this new plan was seen as an alternative to those agreed upon with the crime syndicate, and it was authorized. In order to carry it out, the CIA provided two pistols with silencers, which it passed to the plotters via agents in another European embassy accredited in Havana. The CIA also sent money and new instructions for the network. It wanted each group to be more compartmentalized, and provided them with means of communication to increase their security.

Matamoros could not contain his joy. The moment had arrived to show his new bosses everything that he had learned as a *casquito* in Batista's army.

The month of August 1962 arrived, and Alberto Cruz and María Leopoldina Grau were informed of the plans to provoke an uprising in the nation's capital. They quickly went to see their man in El Recodo Cafeteria, to arrange the final details of the assassination of Commander Ameijeiras. Nevertheless, fate played a trick on them. The traitor who had worked there had fled the country in July, only a few days earlier. He had been afraid of an invasion of Cuba by the U.S. military, and preferred to wait in the United States until it was all over. The pistols were hidden in Herminia Suárez's safe house, and the conspirators continued stalking the Hotel Havana Libre.

It wasn't until March 1963 that they got their opportunity. One night Fidel entered the hotel cafeteria while Santos de la Caridad was on duty. He asked for a chocolate shake, which was obligingly prepared by Santos. Nobody noticed that he opened the door of the refrigerator and slid his hand back to the coil which hid the lethal capsule. He tried to take it out with his fingers, but the effects of freezing made it cling to the metal; he used a little more pressure and the capsule broke open, spilling its lethal contents down the wall of the refrigerator.

Fidel drank his shake, thanked Santos, and left. Perhaps this was the closest that the enemies of the country ever came to consummating the assassination. They would never again have such an opportunity.

Some time later the networks were broken up, the spies arrested, the details were revealed of the planned assassination of Fidel Castro, and the guns and the remaining capsules were confiscated. And so ended that one adventure of the Mafia and the CIA and their attempt to assassinate the Prime Minister of Cuba.[78]

---

[78] Report from Cuban State Security. July 1965.

CHAPTER 10

Special operations

One of the first measures taken by the Special Group (Augmented) of the National Security Council was to remove the main CIA leaders responsible for the Bay of Pigs defeat. In November 1961, Allen Dulles was replaced by John McCone, and several months later Richard Helms took over Richard Bissell's job as deputy director.

Time had also run out for a number of lesser Agency officials. Some were given desk jobs, others retirement. The new Cuban project required men of action and the human and material resources that would commit the Kennedys to supporting intervention in Cuba.

Task Force W was organized in the heart of Langley and headed up by William Harvey, who was in charge of directing the overall Cuban operation. Meanwhile, in Florida, Theodore Shackley and Gordon Campbell were designated first and second in command of the largest U.S.-based operation contrived against a foreign country that ever existed. The CIA's base of operations in Miami, code-named JM/WAVE, came to have an annual budget of $100 million, close to 400 U.S. officers and more than 3,000 Cuban agents and collaborators. All of the Agency's main stations abroad had at least a couple of case officers to gather intelligence and draw up concrete plans against functionaries and installations in Cuba. All this material was sent to JM/WAVE for processing and analysis.

The base of operations was transferred from Coral Gables to the abandoned Richmond Naval Air Station in the southern part of the Miami area. A sign at the entrance told unexpected visitors that they had arrived at Zenith Technical Enterprises, a facade created by the heads of Mongoose.

The structure adopted had various sections: operations, in charge of managing the agents and the marine and air units; personnel, which handled the U.S. employees; logistics, in charge of the purchase and allocation of supplies; cover, which prepared cover stories and fronts; real estate, which bought the properties the other sections required; training; communications and intelligence.

In order to offer its employees cover jobs and to provide the operations with commercial facades, the CIA created countless fake companies and corporations. There were 55 in all, from market analysts to travel agencies, from repair shops to fishing companies, from weapons dealers to real estate agencies, etc.

The case of Radio Swan is a good example of the complex of corporations that were sometimes created. In September 1961, the main office of Gibraltar Steamship Corporation, the parent corporation of the radio station, moved from New York to the Langford Building in the center of Miami. There, they boldly changed the name of the company to the Vanguard Service Corporation. Months later, Radio Swan also vanished, only to reappear as Vanguard Radio America or Radio America, as it was known: the same dog with a different collar.

In order to transport commando groups and to infiltrate them into Cuba, the CIA acquired a fleet of specially-prepared boats which were docked in Homestead, not far from JM/WAVE. The boats were registered in the name of Ace Cartography Company, Inc., supposedly a marine survey firm. The "directors" of this corporation were William A. Robertson and Grayston L. Lynch, the first U.S. citizens to land on the coasts of the Bay of Pigs alongside the mercenaries.

As Mongoose involved continuous incursions for sabotage and terrorism, the CIA recruited Cuban exiles as frogmen for underwater demolition teams. These "recruits" were employed by a ghost company called Marine Engineering and trained with a monthly salary ranging from $275 to $325 when they went on missions.[79]

The veteran operatives from the Bay of Pigs were reactivated, including Frank Sturgis, who was put in charge of a operation called "Study Flights." His mission consisted in flying over a preestablished route in Cuban air space in order to activate the coastal defense system. The electronic signals produced as a result of these alerts were then monitored by two U.S. spy ships, the *Oxford* and the *Pocono*, which patrolled off the coasts of the island.

While the operatives were busy in southern Florida, at the headquarters in Langley a technical team was working on all manner of measures to strangle Cuba's economy. These ranged from blocking foreign credits and contaminating sugar to putting pressure on European producers to stop selling their goods to the island. The British bus factory Leyland received a request to sabotage the shipment of vehicles which was waiting on the docks.

In April 1962, the CIA was unhappy with the Cuban exile leaders. There were almost daily squabbles for the favors of the Agency; but even more scandalous was the way in which they appropriated for private use resources which were supposed to be destined for the clandestine struggle they claimed to be conducting in Cuba.

That same month, the CIA sent various leaders recruited to activate the organizations and rebel bands which still survived on the island. However, at this time the possibility could not be discounted that these men would be quickly captured by the G-2. The level of efficiency of the Cuban State Security Department had increased considerably in recent months, and that worried them.

They began to construct elaborate contingency plans in case the scheme to revitalize the internal opposition should fail. They

---

[79] Warren Hinckle and William Turner, *The fish is red: The story of the secret war against Castro.* (New York: Harper & Row, 1981), 115-117.

had many agents in different parts of Cuba, and sufficient information to plan their own compartmentalized structures with cadres at all levels who had some basic preparation in the arts of subversion and terrorism. They would be given the job of developing the plans for the popular uprising which was the key to Mongoose.

In this way the era of the great subversive networks in Cuba was born. It sprang from a program of infiltration of political agents into areas carefully selected for their lack of sociocultural development, and above all for the past influence of political *caciques* who had since become agents. What followed was the meticulous process of recruiting deputy agents who, once approved by Miami, would be spirited away to the training camps in Florida.

Meanwhile, the CIA's fleet sent in tons of weapons, munitions, explosives, and even specialists in military training. Schools for terrorists were set up in secluded areas of Pinar del Río, Las Villas and Oriente. Once all the details were in order, the signal would be given for the uprising and the "betrayed" Cuban people would join the so-called popular revolt, which was really nothing more than a pretext for U.S. military intervention.

Among all these networks, there was one in particular which came very close to achieving its objectives. This was the United Western Front (FUO), created in mid-1962 by the CIA agent Esteban Márquez Novo, alias Plácido. It was based in Pinar del Río, although it had branches that extended into Havana and Matanzas. Before it was completely broken up in 1964, it had been able to organize more than 1,000 subagents into a powerful underground structure backed by considerable resources and the deep trust of the United States.

Márquez Novo organized the FUO into eight territorial commands, and three general ones: intelligence, training, and support. Each territorial command was divided into two sections: one civil, charged with communication, receiving supplies, vigilance, and collecting information; and the other, military, responsible for training the action groups, hiding the weapons and military supplies, and making the plans for the uprising.

At the time they were wiped out, 207 automatic weapons were taken from them, along with more than 25,000 projectiles, 46 pistols, hundreds of hand grenades, 256 sticks of C-4 plastic explosive, and 1,576 other items which included incendiary devices, mines, timers, etc. Six modern radio sets, which the commands had used for contacting each other and JM/WAVE, were also confiscated.

Márquez Novo killed himself when he was about to be captured. However, his second in command, Luis García Menocal Sigle, surrendered to Cuban authorities and told them in great detail about the structure and the plans of the FUO. The following passages are some the most important parts of his declarations:

Around the middle of 1960 an organization sprang up in Pinar del Río called the Constitutional Recovery Movement (MRC), the head of which was Esteban Márquez Novo, an old military man from the regular army. This group was dedicated to propaganda against the revolution and raising funds for an armed uprising in the mountains of that province. Once Márquez Novo obtained the money he needed, he organized an uprising in Lomas del Toro. . . . After about 40 days the band was surrounded by the militia, and almost everyone was captured except the leader, who escaped with a few of his subordinates.

Márquez Novo asked for asylum in the Argentine embassy, and once he was granted it, headed for that country, with a stopover in Venezuela where he was recruited by the CIA on a visit to the U.S. embassy in Caracas. A few days later he traveled to Miami where he was met by a CIA official whose code name was Otto. . . . From there he was taken to a safe house where he was trained, along with another Cuban named Napoleón, who was to be the radio operator . . . .

One dark night in March 1962, a CIA boat called the *Rifle* left its mother ship and sailed to the mouth of the San Diego River on the south coast of Pinar del Río carrying

Esteban and Napoleón, along with cargo which included two RS-1 radios, portable generators, military supplies such as machine guns, 45 caliber pistols, explosives, ammunition, etc. Both took a canoe and followed the river inland for a couple of kilometers until they found an appropriate place to hide the canoe and the materials. . .

Esteban Márquez Novo's mission was to create a spy and subversion network, so that at a determined moment, after having received sufficient matériel, was to sow chaos and destruction in support of an invasion from abroad. While this plan was being forged, the network was to obtain as much political and military information as possible, which would be transferred to the United States by means of the radio equipment. . . . Sheltered in the tranquillity of one of the safe houses, Márquez Novo dedicated himself to political and training work, in order to lay down the ideological base for the organization and improve [the collection of] information.

He wrote a booklet entitled "25 points for a government in arms," and another called "Vigilance and espionage." In the first he expounded on what he thought should be done in the administrative sphere once his cause had triumphed; and in the second he compiled a series of ideas for improving the search for and the gathering of information. . . . He also decided to change the name of his network, selecting the United Western Front, which was used until the end . . . .

The FUO was handicapped almost from the beginning, even apart from its empty ideology. Sooner or later it would be destroyed, and Márquez Novo knew it. He learned too late that the methods he employed were incorrect. Therefore, two years after his infiltration into Cuba, he realized that his creature had become a monster, already almost completely out of his control. Desperate, disheartened and exhausted from a hard struggle he now saw as useless, he sent a message to Otto:

Today is the second anniversary of the founding of the FUO, and I am confident that my labors during this time have been of some use to our cause. . . . A toast, a toast with whiskey or champagne, while I and my men dry our tears with blood-soaked handkerchiefs. . . . Colonel Plácido. [80]

In March 1962, another important intelligence and subversion network began to take shape in the central provinces of the country. Mariano Pinto Rodríguez and Luis Puig Tabares — the former a public prosecutor and the latter the Belgian consul in the city of Cienfuegos — were its leaders. The intelligence organization, which functioned until the second half of 1963, included nearly one hundred collaborators, recruited from former large landholders, military men and public officials. Through them hundreds of economic, political and military reports were received and passed on to the CIA. They also organized a supply channel for Adalberto Méndez Esquijarrosa and his bandits in the north of Las Villas Province. This route was given the code name "Rat Line." The organization was closely connected with other groups including the Constitutional Democratic Legion, the Christian Democratic Movement, the Cuban Internal Resistance, the Magisterial Anticommunist Front, and the Democratic National Front.

One of the messages sent in mid-1962 by a CIA official known as Williams to Mariano Pinto expressed the following about their work:

. . . in spite of the information given to the public, here as well as there, our struggle continues according to plan, and the hour approaches when we can give both of them a glimpse of the fall of the present regime. . . . neither you nor I can afford another Bay of Pigs; this time we cannot fail and we shall not fail. All this requires much time and much patience to ensure that we shall not be fooled, believing that

---

[80] Declarations by Luis García Menocal Sigle to Cuban State Security on the FUO and Esteban Márquez Novo. 1965.

the resistance is greater than it actually is. This time we shall construct a powerful resistance from nothing, and we must make sure that it functions as an efficient machine. . . . in spite of what the press and the radio say with regard to official policy, it is frequently a mask to hide our real intentions, which should be materialized in a clandestine way. . . .[81]

In his statement, agent Luis Puig Tabares explained how the communications functioned between the network and the CIA center in Miami:

> . . . the Belgian diplomats, Ambassador Louis Couvreur and First Secretary Henry Beyens, knew of my work as a CIA agent in Cuba and they facilitated communications with the case officer, Mr. Williams, allowing me to send and receive messages, materials and spy equipment through the Belgian embassy's diplomatic pouch. . . .
>
> Mr. Couvreur and Mr. Beyens gave me materials and equipment sent by Mr. Williams and saw and knew what they were going to be used for. These materials were marine charts of the north coast of Las Villas, compasses and infrared paper to aid in receiving infiltration teams and war matériel at night; receivers, code books and everything we needed to carry out the activities we were engaged in. They also knew all of the instructions the CIA sent, since they came in open envelopes. . . .[82]

Another highly-placed CIA agent, Vicente Munero Rojas, arrested in Havana in 1964, told of his subversive movements in the service of the Agency in 1962:

---

[81] Report from the Cuban State Security Department on the CIA network of Mariano Pinto Rodríguez. 1964.

[82] Declarations by Luis Puig Tabares to Cuban State Security. 1965.

. . . at the end of 1961 I traveled legally to the United States on the pretext of visiting friends. At the Miami airport I was interrogated by immigration authorities, and I informed them of my desire to aid the cause of liberating Cuba. . . Later I was taken to the camp at Opa-Locka where I was visited by two CIA officials who were interested in my motivation and my level of commitment. . . . They sent me to the Tamiami Hotel where I was visited by another case officer named John, who later moved me to a safe house in Coral Gables where I was trained in organizing groups, intelligence, sabotage, communication, etc. . . .

In early 1962, when I returned to Cuba, one of the first missions I completed was to report on the state of the counterrevolutionary organizations and the possibilities of an armed uprising against the government. . . . I formed my own group, the Cuban Patriotic Organization (OPC), recruiting various persons whose political positions I was familiar with. Later, they were very useful to me when the Miami Center sent me sabotage materials to destroy urban transportation in the capital and torch the paper factory known as the Papelería Nacional de Puntas Grandes, as part of an operation that the Americans informed me would topple the government in late 1962. . . .[83]

On May 28, 1962, Pedro A. Cameron Pérez left Key West as a member of a special commando group which also included the agents Joaquín Escandón Ranedo, Luis Nodarse, Radamés Iribar Martínez and Rafael Bonno Ortíz. Their mission was to organize guerrilla centers in the mountains of Oriente Province, promising them economic resources, weapons and anything else they needed once the proper conditions had been created.

The trip, which they made aboard a CIA vessel as a "mother ship," took six days. They arrived at a point just west of the U.S. Naval Base in Guantánamo. On June 4, they disembarked at a place called Playa Arroyo la Costa, which they had previously

---

[83] Declarations by Vicente Munero Rojas to Cuban State Security. 1964.

selected from aerial photographs. After burying the arms and other matériel, they walked almost three days to the place selected for the rendezvous, a farm belonging to Iribar Martínez. Once they had settled in there, they began the intensive labor of trying to convert the campesinos of the country to their cause and convince them to form an anti-government guerrilla unit. With this accomplished, on June 12, the head of the group, Joaquín Escandón, returned to Miami, sneaking out of the country from a place known as Boca de Dos Riós, in the El Aserradero area of the municipality of El Cobre. Two months later, the CIA sent for the rest of the commando unit, to verify Escandón's reports. A rubber raft carried the group from the same part of El Aserradero to a ship flying a U.S. flag which was waiting a few miles off the coast.

As soon as they arrived in the United States, the CIA questioned them about the situation in Cuba and the potential for promoting a guerrilla war. A CIA official promised them that they would soon receive sufficient aid to arm 5,000 men. They agreed that the plans would be carried out no later than February 1963. In December, the same case officer told them to return to Cuba and select the points along the coast where the arms and explosives might be smuggled in and the spots in the mountains for air drops.

On November 14, agents Cameron Pérez and Manuel del Valle Caral left Florida aboard the *Rex*, under the command of Captain Alejandro Bru, and landed at El Aserradero. Shortly thereafter, on December 28, the spies were arrested in a joint operation by Cuban State Security and the Rebel Army; their weapons were confiscated, and the subversive plans of the Central Intelligence Agency were once again frustrated.[84]

One of the major setbacks for the CIA in those months was the failure of the so-called Operation Cupid II in the ominous days of the October Crisis. On November 5, 1962, their agents Miguel Orozco Crespo and Pedro Vera Ortíz were arrested in the

---

[84] Report from Cuban State Security. 1962.

Malas Aguas Farm in the municipality of Viñales in Pinar del Río Province.

Interrogations revealed that Orozco Crespo was head of the CIA Special Missions Group that reached Cuba on October 20. The objectives of that group had been to bury somewhere along the coast half a ton of weapons destined for a subversive network that operated in the province; to carry out military reconnaissance, searching for a supposed Soviet base in the area; and to provide support for another infiltration team of five commandos, under the command of Reynaldo García, who had been sent to detonate explosive charges in the nearby mines of Matahambre.

In order to carry out this operation the two groups had been transferred from Miami to a place called Summerland Key, where they studied maps of their point of disembarkation and awaited final instructions. Then they boarded vessels named *Vilaro*, *Ree-Fee* and *Jlutas*, to take them to the prearranged place. The following day the *Ree-Fee* was to pick up the first four men who had gone to bury the arms, and then make periodic trips to the coast to collect men as they completed their tasks.

November 7 was the date selected for the two groups to rendezvous in a place called Loma Pelada, where a helicopter would land to transfer them to a ship waiting some distance offshore. Should anything go wrong, they were to take refuge in a number of preestablished safe houses and then send a coded message to Miami, in order to coordinate their rescue.

Orozco opted to tell all he knew from the beginning, unabashedly declaring that he had carried out 25 similar missions in Cuba that year. His bosses in Florida were the CIA officials Rip Robertson and Robert Wall, the latter a personal friend of the Kennedys.

The immediate plans of the Special Missions Group included training the Alpha 66 counterrevolutionary organization and recruiting 150 more men to improve the effectiveness of the group. They were also planning a major act of sabotage at a nickel processing plant in Oriente Province.

Orozco supplied other important information, alerting Cuban authorities to a top secret operation whose objectives were to militarily take over Cayo Romano on the north coast of Camagüey Province in order to establish an alternative government there. At the same time an attack was to be launched against Puerto Cabezas, Nicaragua — in coordination with Nicaraguan dictator Anastasio Somoza — to give the appearance of a Cuban reprisal for that country's collaboration with the United States in the preparations for the Bay of Pigs invasion. The situation created by a Cuba-Nicaragua conflict, added to the establishment of a provisional government on the island, would be the new pretext for a U.S. action against Cuba.

Once again the Mongoose plans were frustrated. The CIA lost its chief of special missions, and even worse for them, they lost the chance to carry out an operation which would have given them their long-awaited excuse. Cuba's public exposure of Miguel Orozco's group and their plans, coming so soon after the Missile Crisis, must surely have convinced the strategists in Washington that Mongoose was not a viable proposition and that they would need new ideas and new people to implement them if they were to continue their war against the Cuban revolution.[85]

In those early years, the fledgling Cuban State Security system was constantly vigilant and alert, making use of the intelligence and the bravery of an entire nation. Lacking both a long history and combat experience, they were nevertheless able to uncover in time the constant flow of new subversive plans from the north and impede the many acts of aggression by the U.S. empire.

Today, Cuba now has a mature intelligence organization, always alert, a veteran force, schooled in the latest techniques, which has trained a new generation with the greatest of rigor, ever-vigilant to defend our achievements and social gains.

The cases mentioned here are only a small sample. Other important battles have also been fought and continue to be fought

---

[85] Declarations by Miguel Orozco Crespo to Cuban State Security. November 1962.

daily, although sometimes the passage of time is necessary in order to be able to relate them objectively, with all of the material from both parties involved in the struggle.

Epilogue

In January 1963, Operation Mongoose was officially "discontinued." So stated an official memorandum issued by General Edward Lansdale to the Assistant Secretary of Political Affairs for the U.S. State Department. Nevertheless, the plans to destabilize Cuba were far from over.

Task Force W, JM/WAVE and the other structures generated during those years had built new projects and operations for the purpose of creating political and military conditions in Cuba which would encourage an "open revolt of the people." The principal task was, and still is, to recruit disaffected elements to form an internal opposition which would present to the rest of the world an image of dissidence and social strife, serving as a prelude to an armed intervention.

Assassination attempts, terrorists acts, sabotage, infiltration, propaganda campaigns, economic blockade, psychological warfare, economic destabilization, bacteriological warfare, pirate attacks, and aggression and provocation from the U.S. Naval Base at Guantánamo, have been the essence of the operations carried out by the United States government throughout all these years.

More than any of the episodes related so far, the incidents that took place in 1962 will go down in history as the turning point, where civilization as we know it was on the verge of disappearing due to the obstinacy of the most powerful nation on earth. This dramatic moment will always be remembered for the gallantry with which Cuba defended the right to choose its own path, in spite of the imminent danger to the island of nuclear annihilation.

There has probably never been another occasion which better demonstrated the lengths to which the Cuban people would go to defend their dignity and sovereignty, establishing the precedent that has formed the basis of Cuba's position in today's unipolar world: resist and overcome.

The Missile Crisis exposed the hypocritical character of U.S. policy; the world now had conclusive proof that imperialist maneuvers were based upon "plausible deniability," acting above the law and disregarding the rights of others. Although these were not the only years during which the true nature of Washington's policy was exposed, the period between 1959 and 1962 was nonetheless crucial in this respect.

The year 1963 brought with it new battles which constantly hardened the Cuban people in the struggle. From very early on that year, more attempts on the life of Fidel Castro were in preparation, not to mention the most surprising conspiracy of all — the assassination of President John F. Kennedy — in which it appears that the same minds did the planning and the same hands pulled the trigger.

Chronology

1959

January 1

Troops under the command of Che Guevara take Santa Clara and Batista flees to the Dominican Republic. Revolutionary forces take control of Havana, and Fidel Castro and his Rebel Army seize Santiago de Cuba, the nation's second largest city. The revolution has triumphed.

January 7

The United States recognizes the new government. Nevertheless, as will be revealed years later, the U.S. administration has already begun to harass the new Cuban authorities.

January 10

Earl Smith resigns as U.S. ambassador in Cuba. He is replaced by Philip Bonsal.

January 16

Cuba asks the United States to return war criminals from the Batista regime who have taken refuge in the United States, so that they may stand trial.

January 16

Announcements are made recruiting mercenaries in Santo Domingo to land on the coast of Cuba "as soon as opposition to the revolution arises."

January 21

A mass demonstration occurs outside the Presidential Palace in Havana denouncing the United States for giving sanctuary to war criminals and embezzlers of public funds. Fidel Castro gives a speech condemning U.S. intervention in the internal affairs of Cuba. More than 300 Latin American journalists cover the rally.

January 27

The U.S. grants asylum to well-known assassins associated with the Batista dictatorship.

February 1

A meeting is held between Frank Bender, the Dominican dictator Rafael Leónidas Trujillo and Johnny Abbes García to analyze the plans they are hatching against the Cuban revolution.

February 2

U.S. citizen Allen Mayer is arrested on a private plane after landing illegally in Cuba for the purpose of assassinating Fidel Castro.

February 11

The *New York Times* reports that the Cuban Ministry of State has announced the withdrawal of the U.S. military troops which trained Batista's armed forces.

February 13

Prodded by the United States, Cuban Prime Minister Jose Miró Cardona resigns. Fidel Castro takes over his post.

March 10

The U.S. National Security Council meets in secret session to discuss how to install a new government in Cuba.

March 26

The Cuban police uncover a plot to assassinate Fidel Castro. The plot revolves around Rolando Masferrer and Ernesto de la Fe, Batista supporters in exile in the United States.

April 15

William Morgan travels to Miami to meet with Colonel Augusto Ferrando, Dominican consul in that city. Also present are Frank Boscher and Manuel Benítez who explain the plots against Cuba and make available a million dollars provided by Trujillo to overthrow Fidel Castro.

April 15

Members of the first counterrevolutionary cell uncovered since the triumph of the revolution are arrested in Regla. They are part of an organization with foreign contacts financed by elements of the Batista regime.

April 17

Two U.S. citizens are caught in the act of trying to photograph the interior of La Cabaña Fortress, in clear violation of established laws.

May 2

Cuba signs a four-point agreement with the United States for technical cooperation in the development of agrarian reform.

May 3

William Morgan returns to Miami and speaks to Trujillo via telephone. He is told about Father Ricardo Velazco Ordóñez' visit to Cuba.

May 12

A meeting of U.S. ambassadors in South America is held in Chile, where they agree on a plan against the Cuban government which includes exerting pressure on the other governments of the region and unleashing a slander campaign and attacks against Cuba in the pro-U.S. press.

May 17

The Agrarian Reform Law is passed, establishing a limit on the amount of land one person can hold and confiscating the rest, compensating the owners and distributing the excess land amongst the peasants who work it. Seventy five percent of the arable land was in the hands of foreigners. Five U.S. companies owned or controlled more than two million acres in Cuba.

June 2

The government of the Dominican Republic recruits fascist elements and thugs for the purpose of creating a so-called foreign legion to carry out provocations and adventures in Cuba and Central America.

June 4

Father Velazco arrives in Cuba where he meets with William Morgan, Eloy Gutiérrez Menoyo, Arturo Hernández and Dr. Armando Caiñas Milanés.

June 6

Eleven persons were detained in Santiago de Cuba for conspiring against the revolution. Among them were several former members of the military.

June 7

The Cuban embassies in Haiti and the Dominican Republic are attacked by counterrevolutionaries and Batista supporters.

June 10

The car belonging to the Cuban ambassador to the Dominican Republic is riddled with bullets, wounding the driver. The car was hit 56 times. This action was directed by Roberto Martín Pérez and Esteban Ventura.

June 16

Cuba rejects the U.S. terms for compensating expropriated land and offers 20 year bonds at 4.5% interest. (In 1958 bonds in the United

States paid approximately 3.8% interest.) The landlords refused to accept the compensation because the value of the land was based on the figures they themselves had declared for tax purposes.

June 17
Cuban Minister of Foreign Affairs Raúl Roa accuses Dominican dictator Trujillo before the OAS of plotting against Cuba.

June 20
Father Velazco, William Morgan, Arturo Hernández, Ramón Mestre and others hold their final meeting at Havana's Hotel Capri. They agree on a possible date for smuggling weapons into Cuba.

June 24
Counterrevolutionary Alberto Palacio Sablón is detained for possession of several homemade bombs. Other coconspirators are later captured.

June 26
Cuba severs diplomatic relations with the Dominican Republic.

June 28
A small yellow and white plane takes off from the United States and drops parachutes with military equipment over Consolación del Sur. They are picked up by the Rebel Army.

July 2
In Miami, William Morgan receives from Dominican consul Augusto Ferrando a yacht loaded with weapons to be used by counterrevolutionaries in Cuba.

July 3
Eight counterrevolutionaries are arrested and a large quantity of weapons, bombs and explosives destined for sabotage and assassination attempts is confiscated.

July 4
The Cuban consul in Miami is attacked by counterrevolutionary Batista supporters.

July 14
A cargo plane belonging to the Cuban Armed Forces is hijacked and flown to the United States.

July 15
Several counterrevolutionaries are arrested in Guanajay after an assassination attempt on the life of a Rebel Army officer.

July 19
The Investigation Department of the Rebel Army (DIER) arrests a group of conspirators who operated in Marianao and other areas of Havana.

July 22

A group of counterrevolutionaries who attacked a military unit from an auto and then fled are captured in Havana.

July 26

A Cessna plane from the United States is downed in Jaruco. The pilot is traitor Rafael del Pino, one of the founders of the "White Rose" counterrevolutionary organization.

August 5

Four planes are destroyed in the Air International Corporation hangar in Miami as part of a plan to sabotage Cuban economic interests, especially air travel between Cuba and the United States. These planes had been purchased by the Batista government and remained in Florida. These actions were carried out with the approval of Senator Eastland and the Internal Security Sub-committee of the U.S. Senate.

August 5

Members of the Investigation Department of the Rebel Army capture counterrevolutionary elements in Camagüey who were planning to attack a prison in that province to break out war criminals being held there. Their weapons are confiscated.

August 8

Two officials from the U.S. embassy in Havana are arrested while leading a meeting of counterrevolutionary elements preparing sabotage and other activities. Both are expelled from the country.

August 8

The National Revolutionary Police discover that American National Life, one of the largest insurance companies in Cuba, is making economic contributions to support the plans of counterrevolutionary agents, Trujillo's followers, and their U.S. instigators.

August 8

Fourteen counterrevolutionaries, members of the White Rose, are detained in Pinar del Río after confessing involvement in a plot which was spread throughout the entire province as well as Candelaria and Artemisa. Their objective was to coordinate their activities with foreign elements so that they might act jointly at the opportune moment.

August 10

Radio transmissions from the Dominican Republic exhort Cubans to take up arms, and Cuba confirms the existence of a counter-revolutionary plot based in Santo Domingo.

August 11

Hundreds of former soldiers of the Batista government are detained after being implicated in a vast plan to regroup the members of the old army and police force, big landholders, embezzlers and others to support the landing of mercenaries from Santo Domingo, incite armed uprisings in the capital and assassinate leaders of the revolution.

August 11

A Dominican plane drops several parachutes with military equipment in the Escambray mountains.

August 12

A Dominican plane lands in Trinidad with weapons and military supplies for the counterrevolution. Aboard the plane is Father Velazco, who has come to meet with leaders of the conspiracy and assess the situation in the territory.

August 13

The capture of another of Trujillo's planes, the confiscation of its cargo, and the arrest of its crew puts an end to the conspiracy scheme of the Dominican dictator backed by the CIA.

August 19

Several Batista supporters, fugitives from revolutionary justice who had taken up arms in the Pan de Azúcar region of the Cordillera de los Organos mountains of Pinar del Río, are captured.

September 21

A conspiracy is uncovered involving ex-military personnel of the Batista dictatorship. Forty persons who planned terrorist attacks against the airport, the Toa weapons depot and other sites are captured.

October 9

A gray steel twin engine plane from the United States drops five parachutes with military supplies into the Aguacatales area, near the town of Minas de Matahambre in the province of Pinar del Río. Rebel Army forces confiscate all of them.

October 9

Eight counterrevolutionaries are arrested in Mariel as they try to leave for the United States for the purpose of organizing an expedition to land on the Pinar del Río coastline and then move inland into the Pan de Azúcar region.

October 12

An unidentified plane flies over the town of San Gabriel, between Güira and Quivicán, but is repelled by Rebel Army forces.

October 18
"El Cabo" Lara, head of the bandits who laid waste to extensive rural areas in Pinar del Río Province, is captured.

October 19
Several planes proceeding from the United States bombard and machine gun areas in the western part of Cuba.

October 19
Commander Camilo Cienfuegos arrests the traitor Huber Matos and several of his collaborators who were trying to incite to rebellion the Ignacio Agramonte Regiment in Camagüey.

October 21
Havana is attacked by air, leaving two persons dead and 45 wounded. Pedro Luis Díaz Lanz, who had been head of the Cuban Air Force before deserting to Miami, later admits to the FBI that he had flown to the Cuban capital on that day, but claims that he only dropped pamphlets over the city. Cuba asks for his extradition, but a U.S. judge refuses to issue an arrest order.

October 22
A plane piloted by the nephew of former Colonel Eleuterio Pedraza is shot down as it is preparing to attack areas of Sagua la Grande.

October 22
A plane flying over the America Sugar Mill in Oriente is driven back by Rebel Army forces as it prepares to bomb the region.

October 22
Fidel Castro publicly denounces the plans of Huber Matos and his accomplices to carry out a counterrevolutionary coup d' ètat.

October 22
A passenger train in Las Villas province is machine-gunned from the air. In response to this attack the Cuban Prime Minister announces the formation of the People's Militia.

October 26
A grenade is thrown at the *Revolución* newspaper building.

November 13
The Cuban government sends a note to the United States explaining that the country is being threatened and that since the United States refuses to sell arms to Cuba, the latter will, in order to defend itself, have to acquire them anywhere in the world that it can.

November 18
Various groups of counterrevolutionaries who have been planning assassinations, sabotage and acts of terrorism are arrested in Santiago de Cuba.

Mid-November

The CIA organizes in Miami noted figures from Batista's tyrannical right-wing regime, former members of repressive bodies, criminals and gangsters to form a group called the Movimiento Anticomunista Obrero y Campesino (MAOC) — the Workers' and Peasants' Anti-Communist Movement.

Mid-November

Major Van Horn and Colonel Nichols, of U.S. Military Intelligence, meet in Havana with a Cuban security agent and propose blowing up the oil refinery and the Tallapiedra Power Plant, sending espionage information, and promoting uprisings and attempts on the lives of revolutionary leaders.

December 11

J.C. King, head of the CIA's Western Hemisphere Division, sends a memorandum to Allen Dulles, proposing that he analyze the possibility of eliminating Fidel Castro.

Mid-December

The CIA proposes recruiting exiles and training them in Latin American countries to unleash paramilitary actions against Cuba.

December 30

Members of the Investigation Department of the FAR (DIFAR) uncover a conspiracy of vast proportions headed by the counterrevolutionary Eugenio de Sosa Chabau and the former Batista lieutenant, Antonio Alburquerque Tamayo.

1960

First few days
Various sugar mills and cane fields are attacked from the air with incendiary bombs. Some of the planes are shot down. Two U.S. pilots are captured and three are killed.

January 12
Planes proceeding from the United States set fire to cane fields in Jaruco in Havana Province.

January 13
CIA Director Allen Dulles addresses the Special Group with the idea of a Cuba Project. They form a Cuba Task Force for the purpose of carrying out actions against Fidel Castro's government.

January 20
Planes from the United States set fire to cane fields in Rancho Veloz in Las Villas Province.

January 24
A group of counterrevolutionaries planning to blow up a bridge in Mantua are arrested in Pinar del Río.

January 28
A plane proceeding from the United States sets fire to 15,000,000 arrobas [3,750,000 pounds] of cane in the Adelaida Sugar Mill in Camagüey.

January 29
A twin engine plane, coming from the north, causes the loss of thousands of arrobas of cane in 10 sugar producing areas in Camagüey and Oriente, dropping white phosphorus incendiary bombs.

February 2
A plane drops a wooden receptacle carrying gunpowder and white phosphorus over the Bacunayagua Bridge on the Vía Blanca.

February 18
A plane explodes while trying to bomb the España Sugar Mill. Documents found in the wreckage reveal that Robert Ellis Frost, the pilot who died in the crash, had invaded Cuban territory on three occasions. The U.S. State Department admits that the flight originated in its territory and apologizes.

February 21
A twin engine plane drops bombs on the towns of Regla and Cojímar, hitting an area near an orphanage in the latter.

February 23

A plane flying from the United States drops white phosphorus on cane fields in the provinces of Matanzas and Las Villas.

February 24

A gray twin engine plane raids the Trinidad Sugar Mill.

February 29

Secretary of State John Foster Dulles rejects Cuba's offer to begin negotiations on the condition that the United States take no unilateral action that could damage the Cuban economy while the talks are going on.

March 2

Planes drop white phosphorus on the Washington Sugar Mill in the province of Las Villas and the Chaparra and Delicias Sugar Mills in Oriente.

March 4

La Coubre, a ship bringing weapons from Belgium for the Rebel Army, explodes in Havana Harbor. Seventy-two persons die and more than two hundred are injured.

March 8

A plane flying from the United States drops inflammable materials on sugarcane zones of San Cristóbal and burns more than 200,000 arrobas (50,000 pounds) of cane in the La Verbena colony in Pinar del Río.

March 9

A correspondent for *Revolución* newspaper is attacked by gunfire in the city of Tampa, Florida, in the United States.

March 10

A group of seven counterrevolutionaries is captured at the Rancho Boyeros Airport as they try to hijack a Havana-Santiago passenger plane to fly it to the United States. Two pistols are taken from them.

March 17

President Eisenhower and the Special Group of the National Security Council approve an operation against Cuba proposed by Allen Dulles, with an eye toward organizing and training Cuban exiles for an invasion of the island. The training is to take place in Guatemala. A copy of the plans for the covert action is distributed within the CIA.

March 21

A plane piloted by Howard Lewis and William Shergales is downed in Carbonera, between Matanzas and Varadero.

March 21
Members of a counterrevolutionay group with branches in Placetas and Fomento are arrested in Santa Clara.

March 22
A plane from the United States is captured as it tries to secretly pick up Dámaso Montesinos, a former colonel in the Batista regime.

March-August
The Technical Services Division of the CIA draws up a plan to spray the television studio Fidel Castro used for his speeches with a chemical substance which produces the same effects as LSD. It also prepares operations to contaminate a box of cigars destined for Fidel with a chemical agent which provokes temporary disorientation, and to destroy his beard with thallium salts. None of these projects is carried out.

April
The head of the CIA station in Guatemala, Robert Kendall Davis, negotiates with President Miguel Ydígoras Fuentes regarding the use of the Retalhuleu Ranch, property of Roberto Alejos, as an air base and training camp for the Cuban exiles.

April 2
Planes coming from the north set fire to sugarcane zones of Havana and Matanzas Provinces. Hundreds of thousands of arrobas of cane are lost.

April 4
A plane taking off from Guantánamo Naval Base drops incendiary material on the city of Santiago de Cuba.

April 9
A group of counterrevolutionaries murder a peasant in the Sierra Maestra. Among the criminals is Manuel Beatón, the killer of Commander Cristino Naranjo.

April 23
A plane arriving from the north sets fire to several sugarcane plantations in Bauta.

April 29
A counterrevolutionary conspiracy is uncovered. Weapons, explosives and other materials are confiscated. Among those arrested are Eduardo Suárez Rivas, Sergio Sanjenís Cabarrocas and José Márquez Vega.

May 7
Counterrevolutionaries carry out a dynamite attempt on the building which houses the revolutionary newspaper *La Calle*.

May 7

Cuba and the Soviet Union reestablish diplomatic relations, broken off in 1952 after Batista's coup d'état.

May 11

A group of the members of the Liberación Unida Democrática (United Democratic Liberation) are arrested in Marianao.

May 17

Radio Swan, a CIA radio station directed against Cuba, begins transmitting.

May 21

A small plane piloted by the counterrevolutionary Edward Duque is downed on the Havana-Mariel highway.

May 21

Cuba asks the foreign refineries in its territory — the only ones on the island — to process crude oil imported from the Soviet Union at favorable prices.

May 31

Counterrevolutionary elements driving a car at high speed shoot at the *Revolución* newspaper building.

June 7

When the first shipload of crude oil arrives from the Soviet Union, the Shell, Esso and Texaco refineries (the former a British company, the others U.S. firms) refuse to refine it.

June 15

The counterrevolutionary organization La Cruz (the Cross) infiltrates Mario Tauler Sague and Armando Cubría Ramos into the Punta Hicacos region of Matanzas on a mission to try to assassinate Fidel Castro and to carry out sabotage.

June 16

U.S. diplomats Edwin L. Sweet and William G. Friedman are arrested when they are found at a meeting of Cuban counter-revolutionary conspirators. They were engaged in granting asylum, financing subversive publications and encouraging terrorist acts, including the smuggling of weapons. It is proven that Friedman and his wife are members of the FBI, and according to international law, they are expelled from the country.

June 22

Antonio Varona, Manuel Artime, Justo Carrillo, José Ignacio Rivero and Aureliano Sánchez Arango create in Mexico the Frente Revolucionario Democrático (FRD) [Revolutionary Democratic

Front], an alliance of counterrevolutionary organizations sponsored by the CIA.

June 27

The U.S. Congress begins to promote a clause in the Sugar Act which would eliminate Cuba's sugar quota.

June 28-July 1

The refineries which refuse to refine Soviet oil are nationalized.

July 2

Eisenhower approves a law suspending the purchase of Cuban sugar.

July 5

In response to the attitude taken by the United States in suspending the purchase of Cuban sugar, the Council of Ministers agrees to grant to the President and the Prime Minister of the Republic the power to expropriate and nationalize U.S. properties in Cuba.

July 7

Two CIA agents are killed as they disembark on a beach in Oriente.

July 9

The Soviet Union agrees to purchase the 700,000 tons of sugar that the United States refused to buy.

Mid-July

The CIA coordinates a private meeting between Senator John Kennedy and four Cuban exiles: Manuel Artime, Tony Varona, Aureliano Sánchez Arango and José Miró Cardona for the purpose of informing the presidential candidate that the CIA has a plan to depose Fidel Castro.

July 20

A plan to assassinate Raúl Castro is initiated. Tracy Barnes, second in command to Richard Bissell, deputy director of the CIA, sends a cable to the station in Havana which reads: "Possible removal top three leaders is receiving serious consideration at HQS." The idea is to use a Cuban agent to create an "accident," but in the end, he doesn't find the opportunity to arrange it.[86]

July 23

In the first commercial treaty between the two countries, China agrees to purchase from Cuba 500,000 tons of sugar annually for five years at world market prices.

August 6

U.S. soldiers shoot 14 bursts of machine gun fire at Cuban territory from the Guantánamo Naval Base.

---

[86] *Alleged assassination plots*, 73.

August 16

According to U.S. authorities, the first plot to assassinate Fidel Castro is initiated — the first of at least eight such plots which the Senate would find evidence of in 1975.

August 24

Speedboats bombard the Sierra Maestra Hotel, the Chaplin Theater and a residential area of Miramar.

Early September

Robert Maheu, a CIA agent, meets in Beverly Hills, California with John Rosselli to discuss an attempt to assassinate Fidel Castro. He is offered $150,000 and told that the action is essential for the success of an invasion. Rosselli agrees to participate.

September 8

Battalions of militia are organized under the command of the Rebel Army, in order to eradicate the bands of counterrevolutionaries in the Escambray mountains. The "cleanup" operation begins.

September 8

U.S. citizens including diplomat Marjorie Lennox, Eustace D. Brunet, Edmundo R. Taranski and Daniel L. Carswell are arrested while, under orders from the CIA, they try to place microphones in the offices of the Chinese News Agency Xinhua.

September 18

Fidel Castro arrives in New York to speak to the UN General Assembly. The Technical Services Division of the CIA develops various measures involving explosives and poisons to use in an assassination attempt, but none could be carried out.

September 24

Maheu and Rosselli meet with the chief of the Operational Support Division of the CIA, James O'Connell, to arrange the details of an operation against Fidel Castro. Rosselli, using the pseudonym John Rawlston, presented himself to Cuban contacts as an agent of "some business interests of Wall Street that had . . . nickel interests and properties around in Cuba and I was getting financial assistance from them."[87]

October 4

A group of mercenaries, proceeding from the United States and with the support of the CIA, disembark in Baracoa, in Oriente. The leader of the mercenaries is killed in the act, and 21 are captured, including a U.S. citizen.

---

[87] *Alleged assassination plots*, 76.

October 7
Foreign Minister Raúl Roa denounces the CIA at the UN for training exiles and mercenaries in Guatemala for an attack on Cuba.

October 8
A large quantity of weapons and matériel dropped from a U.S. plane for use by counterrevolutionary groups in the Escambray mountains in Las Villas Province is captured.

October 8
The Rebel Army concludes the first operation known as "Clean Up the Escambray," which puts an end to the CIA's plans for a mercenary brigade to land in the Trinidad region. The main leaders of the counterrevolutionary bands are arrested, including Porfirio Ramírez, Plinio Prieto and Sinesio Walsh.

October 13
Abelardo León Blanco, the Cuban Consul in Miami is seriously injured during a counterrevolutionary attack on the consulate.

Mid-October
The CIA develops a plan to infiltrate groups of Cubans trained by North Americans. The plan is given the code name Operation Pluto. It is eventually converted into a large-scale invasion which will take place at the Bay of Pigs in April 1961.

October 18
Continuing with the plans to assassinate Fidel Castro, Rosselli introduces Maheu to two mafiosos with whom he intends to work: Momo Salvatore Giancana (Sam Gold), who will be the back-up man, and Santos Trafficante (Joe), who is to go to Cuba to make the preparations.

October 19
The United States initiates its embargo on all U.S. goods destined for Cuba.

October 24
In response to the embargo, Cuba nationalizes remaining U.S. properties.

October 29
A DC-3 commercial airplane is hijacked in flight from Havana to Nueva Gerona. One soldier is killed, and the pilot and a 14 year-old boy are injured.

November 18
Allen Dulles and Richard Bissell travel to Palm Beach, Florida, to inform President-elect Kennedy about the CIA's covert plans for an invasion of Cuba.

November 30

Commander Manuel "Piti" Fajardo is assassinated in an ambush carried out by counterrevolutionary elements operating in the Escambray.

December 1

A U.S. rocket explodes over the Holguín area.

December 8

The Ministry of the Revolutionary Armed Forces reports the liquidation of a counterrevolutionary group working out of the Sierra de los Organos in Pinar del Río.

December 26

Saboteurs in the service of the CIA set fire to the Flogar Department Store.

December 31

La Epoca, another Havana store, is practically destroyed by arson.

December 31

The leaders of the Cuban revolution, faced with actions which point to a direct U.S. invasion, order the general mobilization of the people.

1961

January
Early in the Kennedy administration, Richard Bissell discusses with William Harvey the possibility of establishing an "executive action capability" to neutralize foreign political leaders who are hostile to Washington, including assassination as a "last resort." Bissell orders this project to proceed. The Executive Action Group centers its attention almost exclusively on Cuba.[88]

January 1
Cuba initiates its national literacy campaign which, in one year, reduces illiteracy from 25% to 3.9%.

January 2
Cuba formally charges before the UN Security Council that the United States is preparing an invasion of Cuba and that the U.S. embassy in Havana has been carrying out espionage activities. Cuba demands that the number of personnel at the embassy be reduced to 11, the same number that Cuba maintains in Washington.

January 3
The U.S. breaks off diplomatic and consular relations with Cuba and authorizes the Swiss embassy in Havana to manage its affairs.

January 5
Voluntary teacher Conrado Benítez is murdered by counter-revolutionaries while teaching peasants in the Escambray mountains to read and write.

January 7
A band of terrorists following CIA instructions to create a state of alarm in the population is arrested in Havana.

January 7
A weapons drop is made over Pinar del Río and the Escambray from U.S. planes. Soldiers and militia capture the load.

January 9
U.S. weapons are seized in Pinar del Río, between Bahía Honda and Cabañas, after they were dropped from U.S. planes.

January 12
Manuel Prieto Gómez, a Cuban worker at the U.S. Naval Base in Guantánamo is tortured by U.S. soldiers from the installation after they accuse him of sympathizing with the revolution.

---

[88] *Alleged assassination plots*, 83.

January 17

The United States prohibits its citizens from visiting Cuba.

January 19

A landing by mercenaries in the service of the CIA who hope to join bandits operating in Pinar del Río is frustrated.

January 20

The use of a base in the Bahamas against Cuba is denounced. A television documentary is shown on Britain's BBC detailing shipments of arms to Andros Island.

January 20

CIA director Allen Dulles informs the recently elected President Kennedy of plans for an invasion of Cuba.

February 17

An aircraft proceeding from the north with its lights off flies over the Miramar neighborhood of Havana, dropping subversive literature.

February 22

Another voluntary teacher in the literacy campaign, Pedro Morejón Quintana, is murdered.

February 24

CIA agents trained in secret bases in Panama begin to infiltrate Cuba. Their mission is to coordinate the actions of counter-revolutionary organizations in the months prior to the attack at the Bay of Pigs. On this day, Manuel Reyes García enters the country with forged documents, marking the beginning of this operation.

March 7

At a memorial ceremony for the martyrs of *La Coubre*, Fidel Castro announces that the bands of mercenaries in the Escambray have been eliminated.

March 10

The nationalized Ten Cent Store on the corner of Obispo and Monte in Havana is torched by the counterrevolution.

March 11

President Kennedy signs the National Security Act Memorandum (NSAM No. 31), implementing plans for an invasion of Cuba by Cuban exiles.

March 11

Sabotage leaves a large part of Havana without electricity.

March 12

A vessel attacks the Hermanos Díaz oil refinery in Santiago de Cuba.

March 12

At a meeting held at the Hotel Fountainebleau in Miami, John Rosselli, under orders from the CIA, hands Cuban counter-revolutionary Antonio de Varona capsules containing a powerful poison to be used to assassinate Fidel Castro.

March 13

Humberto Sorí Marín and Rafael Díaz Hanscom infiltrate the northern coast of Havana Province as the leadership created by the CIA to direct the internal counterrevolutionary movement.

March 18

Humberto Sorí Marín, Rafael Díaz Hanscom and Rogelio González Corso are captured in the company of the main counter-revolutionary leaders in Cuba, as they are putting the final touches on a terrorist plan which was to have been kicked off on March 27 with the assassination of Fidel Castro.

March 22

The "Political Front" of the Cuban Revolutionary Council is created, expecting to set itself up as a provisional government once the mercenary brigade lands.

March 31

Continuing the policies of former President Dwight D. Eisenhower, President Kennedy approves the suspension of the sugar quota.

April 3

The U.S. government issues a statement about Cuba in which it expresses its determination to support future democratic governments. It warns the Cuban government to cut all ties with the international communist movement.

First two weeks of April

Brigade 2506, made up of 1,400 men, begins moving from a base in Guatemala to Puerto Cabezas in Nicaragua, the launching point for the invasion of Cuba. The CIA's Special Missions Group has by this point infiltrated 35 agents into the island, many of whom have already lost their secret contacts, since the latter have been arrested.

April 12

At a press conference President Kennedy separates himself from any signs that might indicate that the United States is involved militarily with Cuba, stating that any conflict in Cuba is not a conflict between their two nations, but rather among Cubans.

April 13

A huge fire destroys the El Encanto Department Store and takes the life of the prominent revolutionary leader Fe del Valle.

April 15

A group of B-26 bombers, piloted by Cuban exiles, attacks Cuban air bases. The attack, a CIA operation, is meant to pave the way for the Bay of Pigs invasion by crippling Cuba's air power as much as possible. The objectives attacked were the Santiago de Cuba and San Antonio de los Baños airports and the Havana Air Force Base.

April 16

Hours before the invasion of Cuba, the leaders of the Cuban Revolutionary Council are transported by the CIA to a deserted Air Force Base in Opa-Locka, Florida. They are kept there for several days and their only source of information about the attack on Cuba is the radio.

April 16

At the funeral services for victims of the bombing, Fidel Castro proclaims the socialist character of the revolution. Faced with an imminent invasion, he declares a state of alert.

April 17

Mercenary forces backed by the United States begin the invasion of Cuba at the Bay of Pigs.

April 18

Richard Bissell, second in command of the CIA, learning of the delicate military situation which confronts the mercenary brigade, authorizes six U.S. pilots with three B-26 bombers to launch a napalm attack on Cuban troops. Two of these planes are shot down and the body of one of the pilots is recovered, along with identifying documents. Cuba denounces before the world this proof of U.S. involvement in the aggression.

April 19

The mercenary invasion is defeated in less than 72 hours. One hundred and fourteen mercenaries are killed, 1,189 are captured, and 150 are rescued. Communiqué No. 4, signed by Commander in Chief Fidel Castro reports that "forces of the Rebel Army and the National Revolutionary Militia took by assault the last remaining positions which the mercenary invasion force occupied on our national territory."

April 22

President Kennedy orders General Maxwell D. Taylor to carry out an in-depth study of the reasons for the failure of the invasion.

April 24

President Kennedy takes full responsibility for the aggression against Cuba.

April 25

The United States imposes a total embargo on all goods destined for Cuba.

May 1

Antulio Ramírez Ortiz, a U.S. citizen of Puerto Rican origin, acting on orders of the CIA, hijacks a plane and takes it to Cuba in hope of organizing a provocation against the Cuban government.

May 7

A Cuban Navy ship is attacked and sunk by enemy vessels while on patrol. Commander Andrés González Lines and 16 others perish.

Mid-May

Luis Torroella y Martín Rivero is arrested in Santiago de Cuba. His code name, as will be revealed years later by ex-CIA official Philip Agee, is AM/BLOOD.

May 28

A cinema is sabotaged in Pinar del Río while a show attended by many children and teenagers is in progress. Twenty-six children and 14 adults are injured.

June 13

General Maxwell Taylor presents to President Kennedy the results of the investigation into the mercenary invasion fiasco. Taylor recommends that new guidelines be established for political, military, economic and propaganda actions against the Cuban government.

July 4

Counterrevolutionary elements shoot the guard of a Cubana de Aviación plane and force the pilot to take them to Miami.

July 21

The Special Group of the National Security Council (NSC) agrees that "the basic objective toward Cuba was to provide support to a U.S. program to develop opposition to Castro and help bring about a regime acceptable to the U.S."[89]

July 27

The press reveals new plans to attack Cuba, financed by the United States. Counterrevolutionary mercenaries gathered in Haiti were to attack Cuba, providing a pretext for a large-scale U.S. invasion.

August 11

The Cuban Ministry of the Interior divulges a comprehensive plan of aggression prepared by the CIA to be carried out from the

---

[89] *Alleged assassination plots*, 135, 136.

Guantánamo Naval Base and a plot to assassinate Commanders Fidel Castro and Raúl Castro on July 26 of that year, as part of an operation code-named Patty, the purpose of which was to facilitate military aggression by the United States. The weapons which were to have been used in the plan are exhibited.

September 7

The United States Congress approves a measure denying aid to any country which assists Cuba, unless the President determines that this aid is in the national interest.

September 12

A Ministry of the Interior report denounces a high-ranking Falangist priest who, from the church on the corner of Manrique and Salud in Havana, led activities which caused the death of the worker Arnaldo Socorro and the injury of three other persons.

September 29

The counterrevolutionary Dalia Jorge, a member of the MRP, is arrested while setting off incendiary devices in the Sears Store. From her confession, Cuba learned of a plan to assassinate President Castro while he attended a mass rally in the old Presidential Palace.

Early October

Reynold González, the national coordinator of the MRP, is arrested, along with his principal collaborators. His organization was preparing a number of acts of sabotage and assassination attempts which were to have begun on September 29 with the burning of several stores, warehouses and other economic objectives, and culminating on October 4 with an attempt on the life of Fidel Castro and other leaders during a ceremony on the north terrace of the Presidential Palace.

The Cuban press denounces the psychological warfare operation undertaken by the same organization which, oriented by the CIA, had been circulating copies of a false law — supposedly issued by the revolutionary government — which would take the *Patria Potestad* over their children away from parents. Due to this contrived hysteria, thousands of children were sent by their families to the United States as part of Operation Peter Pan.

October 3

Delfín San Sedré, another volunteer teacher, is murdered.

October 5

McGeorge Bundy signs National Security Action Memorandum No. 100 (NSAM 100) entitled "Contingency Planning for Cuba," which instructs the State Department to evaluate the possible courses of action for the United States "in the contingency that Castro would be in some way or another removed from the Cuban scene," and to prepare together with the Pentagon a contingency plan for military intervention should this occur.

October 6

The Special Group of the NSC meets again and is informed that, in addition to the general covert operations plans, "a contingency plan in connection with the possible removal of Castro from the Cuban scene" is being readied.

October 15

Rubén López Sabariego, a worker on the Guantánamo Naval Base, is murdered by a U.S. Marine captain.

Late October

President Kennedy asks General Edward Lansdale to examine U.S. policy toward Cuba and make recommendations. Lansdale proposes that the United States work with the exiles in Operation Mongoose. In order to achieve this objective, Lansdale foresees the development of a leadership and the need to establish a political base among Cubans opposed to Castro. At the same time Lansdale mentioned that he was looking to develop means to infiltrate Cuba successfully and to organize cells and activities inside Cuba.

November 4

A meeting is held at the White House to develop an important covert action program for sabotage and subversion against Cuba. This program receives the name Operation Mongoose. According to notes taken by Robert Kennedy, "My idea is to resolve things on the island through espionage, sabotage and general disorder, carried out and directed by Cubans themselves, with all groups involved except Batista supporters and communists. We don't know if we'll be successful in overthrowing Castro, but in my opinion we have nothing to lose."

A Special Group (Augmented) is created for the sole purpose of overseeing and controlling Operation Mongoose. President Kennedy designates General Lansdale as head of the operation.

November 27

Counterrevolutionaries operating in the Escambray mountains in the service of the CIA murders Manuel Ascunce Domenech, a young literacy teacher, and a peasant named Pedro Lantigua.

November 30

President Kennedy issues a memorandum to Secretary of State Dean Rusk and others involved, officially establishing the covert

Operation Mongoose, aimed at "using our available assets" to "help Cuba overthrow the Communist regime from within the country and institute a new government with which the United States can peacefully coexist."

Late November

William Harvey is again placed at the head of the CIA's Task Force W, which is expected to carry out a broad range of activities, mostly against Cuban ships and planes outside of Cuban territory, such as contaminating cargoes of sugar and using bribery to stem industrial imports.

Early December

A commando group led by Eugenio Rolando Martínez, a Cuban recruited by the CIA, destroys a railroad bridge and a sugar warehouse. They all manage to escape when Rip Robertson arrives in a rubber boat to fetch them. The mission is one of 15 that Martínez has participated in so far.

December 4

President Kennedy extends until June 30, 1962 the prohibition on importing Cuban sugar that had previously been in effect until the end of the present year.

December 4

The United States submits for the consideration of the Inter-American Peace Commission of the OAS a document entitled "The Castro regime in Cuba." It claims that, "Cuba, as the launching point of Chinese-Soviet imperialism within the defenses of the Western Hemisphere, represents under the Castro regime a serious threat to the collective security of the American republics."

December 14

Two CIA pilots disappear during a covert mission to drop pamphlets over Cuban territory explaining ways to carry out sabotage. The action is part of Operation Fantasma, directed by Frank Sturgis as a part of Operation Mongoose.

1962

January
The CIA initiates a plan to offer rewards for the assassination of Cuban leaders. The rewards go as high as a hundred thousand pesos, depending on the rank of the official murdered.

January-March
U.S. bombers, pursuit planes and patrol planes make 182 passes over Soviet merchant ships, the majority of them in waters near Cuba.

January 1
A plane attacks the port of Carraguao in Pinar del Río.

January 2
A group of spies infiltrate near the town of Santa Cruz del Norte.

January 3
A plane attacks the area south of Pinar del Río between Candelaria and Los Palacios.

January 5
Provocations against Cuban positions come from the Guantánamo Naval Base.

January 7
Infiltrated counterrevolutionary elements operating near the city of Camagüey are captured.

January 7
U.S. forces from the Guantánamo Naval Base parade provokingly in advanced state of alert in response to public denunciation by the Cuban government.

January 7
A plane launches its cargo of U.S. weapons over Pinar del Río and Las Villas. All the weapons are captured.

January 11
A vessel attacks the town of Carraguao in Pinar del Río.

January 11
British delegates visiting Havana report that U.S. businesses are obstructing trade between Cuba and Britain.

January 15
A group of counterrevolutionaries try to take by surprise the Cuban yacht *Pretexto*, anchored in Barlovento. They are intercepted by security personnel.

January 17
A group CIA agents infiltrates the area east of the city of Matanzas.

January 18

General Lansdale submits for the consideration of the Special Group (Augmented) the first version of "The Cuba Project," a 32-task plan within Operation Mongoose aimed at causing the downfall of the Cuban government.

January 19

"Task 33" of Lansdale's plan is created: incapacitate Cuban sugar workers through the use of "non-lethal" chemical substances.

January 22

Counterrevolutionary agents land and attack in the area east of the town of Baracoa. They are surrounded and captured.

January 22-31

Instigated by the U.S. government, the OAS votes to expel Cuba from its ranks. Six countries abstain.

January 28

A number of infiltrated agents are arrested in Santiago de las Vegas.

January 28

A band of saboteurs financed by the CIA is discovered trying to paralyze transportation in the capital by destroying the motors of vehicles with chemical products and magnetic mines.

January 30

Bandit chief Braulio Amador Quesada confesses his connection to the CIA and his involvement in the crimes perpetrated against Pedro Lantigua and Manuel Ascunse. He admits that he organized a band to follow the instructions of the United Catholic Anti-Communist Movement (MACU).

February 3

President John F. Kennedy declares a commercial blockade of Cuba which includes extraterritorial measures that prohibit other countries from exporting to Cuba products which contain U.S. technology. Congress approves legislation prohibiting any type of economic aid from the United States to governments which support Cuba. In response to the expulsion from the OAS, the population of Havana gathers in Revolution Square and approves the Second Declaration of Havana, which denounces the neocolonial maneuver.

February 5

Cuba charges before the United Nations that the United States is preparing a large scale aggression. The accusation is presented by Cuba's UN representative, Mario García Incháustegui.

February 7

The U.S. embargo on trade with Cuba goes into effect.

February 10
An aircraft attacks the north coast of Cuba, in Havana Province, east of the capital.

February 13
Another plane attacks Cayo Romano, in the north of Camagüey Province.

February 14
Cuba is expelled from the Organization of American States, in compliance with the resolution passed in Punta del Este, Uruguay.

February 15
The United States amasses forces, including several aircraft carriers, off the Cuban coastline.

February 16
In the United Nations Cuba charges that the United States is preparing an assault on its own Guantánamo Naval Base as a pretext for unleashing its planned aggression; and that at the same time, the United States is organizing a military alliance in the Caribbean to attack revolutionary Cuba.

February 19
A Cuban boat is hijacked in Cojímar.

February 20
Presidential adviser Walter Rostow asks NATO members to consider the OAS decisions when they formulate their policies in relation to Cuba. He asks them to voluntarily refrain from trading in strategic materials and to reduce trade with the island.

February 20
General Lansdale proposes a second version of the Cuba Project, to be carried out as a six-phase program within Operation Mongoose, to culminate in October 1962 with an open rebellion and the overthrow of the Cuban government.

February 21
A counterrevolutionary band carries out an act of sabotage against a school in Remedios, Las Villas.

February 21
A plane attacks the area between Camajuaní and Remedios.

February 26
A ship attacks the port of Caibarién, Las Villas; while a fishing vessel from a cooperative in Las Villas is hijacked.

February 28
The Association of University Students of Guatemala accuses President Miguel Ydígoras Fuentes of conniving with the U.S. State

Department to operate "non-national military bases for action against a neighboring country."

Early March

The Cuban government carries out its third major operation against the bandits in the Escambray and Sierra de los Organos mountains.

March 1

Dean Rusk admits during a press conference that the U.S. government is exerting strong pressure on its NATO allies to take measures against Cuba.

March 4 and 8

Cuban posts are provoked from the U.S. Naval Base in Guantánamo.

March 4

A spy boat patrols the waters north of Cuban territory, between Mariel and Varadero.

March 12

An aircraft attacks the town of Santa Cruz del Norte.

March 12

A group of counterrevolutionaries in the service of the CIA infiltrate through the keys northeast of Caibarién.

March 13 and 14

A secret meeting is held among the foreign ministers of Nicaragua, Guatemala, Venezuela, and Colombia and U.S. Secretary of State Dean Rusk to agree upon plans for an "invasion" of a Central American country, to be attributed to Fidel Castro's forces, but really carried out by U.S.-trained Cuban mercenaries.

March 16

Infiltrated agents operating in Sancti Spiritus are captured.

March 16

In the presence of the Special Group (Augmented), President Kennedy approves the outline for Operation Mongoose, which states, "In undertaking to cause the overthrow of the target government, the U.S. will make maximum use of the indigenous resources, internal and external, but recognizes that final success will require decisive U.S. military intervention."[90]

March 24

The United States extends the blockade to include all ships proceeding from any country whatsoever which contain products of Cuban origin.

---

[90] Guidelines for Operation Mongoose.

March 29
Cuba tries and condemns the Bay of Pigs invaders.
April
Cuban exile leader José Miró Cardona meets with President Kennedy in the White House. According to reports, after the meeting Miró returned to Miami and told his friends that Fidel Castro would soon be ousted.
April 3
A group of counterrevolutionary agents infiltrates the area northeast of Mantua, Pinar del Río, through a place known as Los Arroyos.
April 12
Counterrevolutionaries attempt an attack in the town of Caimanera in Oriente Province.
April 14
Sixty prisoners wounded in the Bay of Pigs invasion are freed and sent to Miami.
April 16
The band of Osvaldo Ramírez, who murdered the teacher Conrado Benítez, is wiped out.
April 19
Operation Quick Kick begins, large-scale maneuvers on the U.S. East Coast simulating an attack on a Caribbean government hostile to the United States. Three hundred aircraft, 83 warships and 40,000 troops take part in the maneuvers. Kennedy boards one of the ships, the aircraft carrier *Enterprise*, to personally inspect the maneuvers.
April 19
The Soviet tanker *Peking* is harassed by a U.S. destroyer and aircraft carriers off the east coast of Cuba.
April 21
William Harvey, head of Task Force W, gives John Rosselli the poison capsules to be used in an attempt on the life of Fidel Castro. The Cuban contact is once again Antonio Varona and his group.
April 22
A Cuban coast guard cutter is attacked by a heavily armed boat near Santa Cruz del Norte. Three Cuban soldiers are killed, and five more are wounded. The well-known counterrevolutionary and CIA agent Justo Carrillo takes responsibility for the action.
April 25
Two counterrevolutionaries are killed in an attempt to penetrate Cuban soil from the Guantánamo Naval Base.

April 27
More than 50 persons are injured as the result of the criminal sabotage carried out at the Cotorro chemical plant by counter-revolutionary elements in the service of the CIA.

April 28
The offices of Prensa Latina in New York are assaulted by counter-revolutionaries, injuring three employees and causing significant property damage.

Early May
The U.S. Treasury Department formally rescinds Cuba's Most Favored Nation trade status.

May 7
The head of the bandits operating in the area around Consolación del Sur, Francisco Robaina — also known as Machete — is killed in a confrontation with soldiers of the FAR and State Security agents. He had committed various murders of peasants and acts of sabotage.

May 12
An armed boat of the counterrevolutionary organization Alpha 66 attacks a Cuban patrol boat, killing three of its five crew members.

May 20
The U.S. government enacts a restrictive measure concerning the luggage of tourists returning from Cuba, to try to keep U.S. citizens from eluding the blockade against the island.

May 20
New provocations by U.S. soldiers from the Guantánamo Naval Base. They throw burning objects and stones.

May
A U-2 spy plane violates Cuban air space. From January to May planes have buzzed more than 150 Soviet ships, and on 20 occasions the U.S. Navy has subjected Soviet sailors to interrogation.

June 7
A vessel attacks a place known as Cayo Güín, in the northern part of Oriente Province; another vessel attacks an area to the east of Baracoa, in Oriente.

June 23
A group of counterrevolutionaries attack and kill militiaman Manuel Aneiro Subirats who is on guard duty at a medical cooperative in San Miguel del Padrón. Another militiaman, Manuel Delgado, is injured.

June 29
CIA agents José Wright Simon and Ardecales Garzón Avalosque are captured. They had entered Cuban territory from the Naval Base in

Guantánamo. Large quantities of explosives and weapons which had been supplied to them by the CIA are confiscated.

July 1 and 2

U.S. spy planes repeatedly violate Cuban air space. The planes fly over Union de Reyes and Punta Seboruco in Matanzas, and Trinidad and Cienfuegos in Las Villas.

July 2

A boat attacks the Batabanó Anchorage, south of Havana.

July 3

Two more violations of Cuban air space occur: one over Guanabo, in Havana Province, and the other over Cayo Largo, in the south.

July 4

The peasants Eustaquio, Ana and Pío Romero are murdered by a band of rebels in the Condado zone of the Escambray.

July 5

Counterrevolutionaries attempt an attack in the town of Caimanera.

July 5

Counterrevolutionaries attempt another attack, this one in the vicinity of the Trinidad-Sancti Spiritus Highway.

July 6 and 7

Cuban territory is fired upon from positions on the Guantánamo Naval Base for four hours straight.

July 7

Once again a violation of Cuban air space, this time by a U.S. plane on a spy mission, is reported. Another plane proceeding from the U.S. repeatedly flies over a Soviet vessel anchored in Havana Harbor.

July 7 and 8

U.S. soldiers assigned to the Guantánamo Naval Base set fire to shrubs on Cuban soil.

July 8 and 9

U.S. soldiers fire from M-14's; some of the shots come close to hitting Cuban sentries.

July 10

Infiltrated counterrevolutionary elements operating near Jaruco, in Havana Province, are captured.

July 10

Four U.S. planes violate Cuban air space. Almost simultaneously, U.S. troops fire from the Guantánamo Naval Base in the direction of Cuban posts, starting a brush fire.

July 11

Provocations from the Guantánamo Naval Base continue.

July 10, 11 and 12

U.S. positions on the Guantánamo Naval Base fire rifles and machine guns into Cuban territory.

July 13

Cuban fisherman Rodolfo Rosell is tortured and murdered aboard his boat five miles from the town of Caimanera, in the waters of the U.S. Naval Base at Guantánamo. As a further provocation, four U.S. military airplanes and two helicopters fly over the cemetery at a low altitude during his funeral.

July 13

Four counterrevolutionary criminals murder Rebel Army corporal Israel Torres Nieves, and wound another soldier, Ismael Celestrín González. Two of the perpetrators are captured.

July 14

Two more U.S. aircraft spy over different part of the island.

July 14

Troops occupying the Naval Base at Guantánamo again fire into Cuban territory bordering the base.

July 15 and 16

Eight more shots are fired at Cuban territory by U.S. soldiers.

July 16

One of the most impressive displays of mass mourning in the history of the town of Güines takes place at the burial of militiaman Porfirio Acosta, who was murdered by counterrevolutionary elements along the coastal highway between Rosario and Güines.

July 17

Juan Falcon, CIA agent and self-proclaimed national coordinator of the Movimiento de Recuperación Revolucionaria (Movement for the Recovery of the Revolution), appears before Cuban television cameras to testify about the assassination and sabotage plans ordered by the Agency for the purpose of destabilizing the country in order to create favorable conditions for U.S. intervention.

July 17

Three U.S. planes on spy missions violate Cuban air space.

July 17

Six shots are fired at Cuban positions from the U.S. Naval Base at Guantánamo.

July 18

Two more U.S. planes fly over different parts of Cuba.

July 18

U.S. soldiers continue firing on Cuban border guards.

July 19

Two infiltrated counterrevolutionary elements who operated in Jaruco in Havana Province are captured.

July 31

Assistant-Secretary of State for Inter-American Affairs Edwin Martin tells *U.S. News and World Report*, "There is absolutely no doubt that the U.S. policy seeks, above all, to isolate Cuba and prevent it from being able to have an impact on Latin America. We want to get rid of Castro and the Soviet communist influence in Cuba, not just Castro."

Late July

General Lansdale orders the Pentagon to prepare a military contingency plan for Cuba, taking into account information from CIA agents operating on the island regarding an imminent uprising by counterrevolutionary groups.

August 1

Seven violations of Cuban air space occur. U.S. soldiers continue shooting at Cuban soldiers from the Guantánamo Naval Base.

August 2

Between 5:00 and 6:00 p.m., a total of 13 U.S. aircraft on espionage flights violate Cuban air space.

August 3

Counterrevolutionaries Roberto Isaac Mendieta and Epifanio Ramaya Guerra were captured. They were part of a group of four who beat up militiaman Celestrín González and killed Corporal Israel López.

August 4

Two new violations of Cuban air space by four U.S. planes.

August 6

Five more U.S. planes penetrate the skies over Cuba for espionage purposes.

August 6

More shots from the Guantánamo Naval Base.

August 7

Three violations of Cuban air space are reported. Six shots are fired from the U.S. base toward Cuban installations.

August 10

The Special Group (Augmented) meets to decide the course of action to follow within Operation Mongoose. Among the various proposals offered is the "Plan B Plus," that would "exert all possible diplomatic, economic, psychological and other pressures to overthrow the Castro-Communist regime. . . ."

August 12

Two more violations of Cuban air space occur.

August 13

Two violations of the island's air space and two of its jurisdictional waters take place.

August 14

During the 11th Central American and Caribbean Games, held in Jamaica, a group of counterrevolutionaries enter that nation as tourists and then provoke various disturbances and assault Cuban athletes. These offenses are repelled with dignity.

August 15

Infiltrated counterrevolutionaries are apprehended in Cumanayagua.

August 15

Four violations of Cuban air space occur.

August 16

Three more violations of Cuban air space on the part of planes from the United States.

August 18

A counterrevolutionary vessel carries out an attack north of Sagua La Grande in Las Villas Province.

August 19

Two more violations of Cuban air space.

August 21

A Cuban soldier is wounded in the eye by a shot from one of the U.S. positions on the Guantánamo Naval Base.

August 22

The British freighter *S. Hill*, loaded with Cuban sugar for the Soviet Union, is the target of sabotage by CIA agents who contaminate the cargo.

August 22

Thousands of tons of Cuban sugar are contaminated in San Juan, Puerto Rico, by CIA agents.

August 22

Four violations of Cuban air space; U.S. planes buzz Cuban fishing vessels.

August 23

National Security Adviser McGeorge Bundy issues Memorandum No. 181, kicking off "Plan B Plus," an expanded variation of Operation Mongoose.

August 24
A plane attacks the area to the east of the capital, along the coast north of Havana.

August 25
The Havana coastline is attacked by armed vessels proceeding from the United States, which fire a number of shots from a 20mm cannon at the Chaplin Theater and residences in the Miramar neighborhood of Havana. Isidro Borjas, Nóbregas and Juan Manuel Salvat claim responsibility for the action. Two planes with U.S. markings guided the vessels to the area and pointed out the targets.

August 27
A U.S. plane violates Cuban territory six kilometers inland over the town of Union de Reyes in Matanzas Province.

August 30
The presence of the spy vessel *Oxford* is reported off the Havana coast. It is visible from the Malecón (the sea wall which runs much of the length of the city of Havana).

August 30
Two violations of Cuban air space are reported in the area of Imías and Trinidad.

August 30
Cuban security forces frustrate a vast subversive plan by the so-called Anti-Communist Liberation Front (FAL) to take various strategic points in the capital and other cities in order to lay the groundwork for U.S. intervention.

January to August
During this period 5,780 counterrevolutionary actions are carried out, of which 716 involve sabotage of important economic objectives.

September 1
The Port of Caibarién is attacked by the counterrevolutionary organization Alpha 66, financed and guided by the CIA.

September 2
The funeral is held for Luis Ruiz Salvador, Luis Abreu Ruiz, Bienvenido Pardillo Artiles, and Rodrigo Quintero (the latter a 16 year-old member of the Union of Young Communists), all workers at a farm in Escambray who were killed on June 12 by bandits. There was evidence that they had been tortured.

September 3
Cuba is excluded from the Latin American Free Trade Association, in clear violation of the statutes of the organization, whose Article

58 specifies that it is open to the rest of the Latin American states. Mexico and Brazil abstain from the vote.

September 3
Four workers are tortured and murdered at the hands of counterrevolutionaries operating in the El Jíbaro zone of Las Villas.

September 3
Soldiers from the Guantánamo Naval Base fire a total of 43 shots in the direction of Cuban positions.

September 3
Three U.S. senators advocate direct aggression against Cuba. George Smathers, Strom Thurmond and Kenneth B. Keating ask the United States to sponsor an international military alliance similar to NATO to deal with the problem of Cuba.

September 7
Cuban ambassador to Mexico, Carlos Lechuga, denounced the training of mercenaries in 14 bases in the Caribbean, namely: the Cobán Basin, Puerto Miguelito, Bengué Viejo, Mehiches, Campo Flores, Santa Rosa de Copán and the Petén area in Guatemala; Corn Island, Bluefields, Puerto Cabezas and El Rancho de la Fundadora in Nicaragua; Punta Mala and Mamintoes in Panama; as well as other camps in Haiti and the Dominican Republic.

September 8
There is a counterrevolutionary infiltration northeast of Sierra Morena in Las Villas.

September 10
A cutter flees to the north after attacking the Cuban boat *San Pascual* and the British *New Lane* off Cayo Francés, 16 miles from Caibarién. The first was hit 18 times; and the second, which had come to take a cargo of sugar to Britain, a total of 10 times.

September 11
The Soviet Union warns that an attack against Cuba or a Soviet vessel could lead to an international conflict.

September 11
A plane attacks east of the capital, along the north coast.

September 14 and 15
U.S. military aircraft violate Cuban territory and international law as they stalk two Cuban merchant vessels.

September 14
The U.S. Defense Department reveals that it is preparing a plan to enlist Cubans in the U.S. Armed Forces and train them in Spanish-speaking units.

Mid-September

U.S. intelligence services receive the first reports of the installation in Cuba of IRBMs and MRBMs (intermediate and medium range ballistic missiles).

September 15

Three members of ANAP (National Association of Agricultural Producers) are taken by surprise and shot by bands of counter-revolutionaries operating in the Escambray. The victims are Romelio Cornelio, head of the Trinidad area; Juan G. González, a provincial inspector; and Antonio Rodríguez, a technical expert.

September 19

NBC broadcasts a program showing Cuban exiles training in Florida and Guatemala under U.S. supervision.

September 19

A U.S. plane violates Cuban air space over the province of Camagüey.

September 19

The Foreign Relations Commission of the U.S. Senate Armed Forces Committee approves a resolution declaring that the nation will use troops if necessary to resist any attempted communist aggression in the hemisphere.

September 25

In the Florida keys, under the direction of ex-Marine Steve Wilson, counterrevolutionary Cubans are prepared to carry out subversive actions against Cuba.

September 26

The U.S. Senate approves a resolution granting the President powers to intervene militarily in Cuba if a threat to the United States is perceived.

September 27

Five CIA agents linked to the Guantánamo Naval Base are arrested by Cuban State Security forces at a home in the Miramar neighborhood of Havana. Large quantities of weapons are confiscated along with subversive plans. The head of the group is Jorge Luis Cuervo y Calvo and the others are Humberto Gómez Peña, Juan Pacheco Ruiz, Eduardo Moharquech Rab and Gregorio Fidel García Huet.

September 28

A group of counterrevolutionaries who had taken up arms in the Rihito area, near the town of Baire in the Jiguaní territory is arrested. They were responsible for the murder of militiaman Angel Bello.

September 30

CIA agents set off pipe bombs in different parts of the Cuban capital.

Late September

U.S. intelligence services come to the conclusion that there is a medium range ballistic missile (MRBM) site in the area of San Cristóbal in Pinar del Río.

A meeting is held behind closed doors in the U.S. State Department where plans are discussed to force other Latin American countries to participate in the plans for aggression against Cuba.

October 1

The Cuban government issues a declaration in response to the joint declaration by the Congress of the United States to "impede by any means necessary, including the use of weapons, the Cuban regime from extending by force its aggressive or subversive activities to any part of this hemisphere." The Cuban government reaffirms the peace proposals, but makes it clear that the Cuban people are prepared to defend their independence.

October 2

A Hemispheric Conference is convoked by the United States in order to rid Cuba of Fidel Castro and Soviet influence. The U.S. State Department pressures 16 Latin American countries to politically and economically isolate Cuba.

October 2

The blockade is again broadened, establishing strict regulations concerning merchant vessels.

October 2

In a place known as Platero, located on the Circuito Norte Highway, in the stretch between Yaguajay and Caibarién, Arnaldo Martínez Andrade, Ibrahim Cruz Oropesa and other members of the counterrevolutionary band which had committed countless crimes in the zone are surrounded and annihilated by the combined forces of the Rebel Army and the National Revolutionary Militia.

October 4

The U.S. government initiates a plan to break off relations with Cuba based on the alleged theft of documents on the part of the Cuban embassy in Buenos Aires. The Cuban government is accused of meddling in the internal affairs of Argentina, but the lie falls apart with the announcement by the Argentine government that the accusation is false.

October 5

Two planes proceeding from the United States violate Cuban air space as they fly over various points in Havana and Matanzas.

October 7

A Neptune P2V from the United States provokes a merchant vessel near the Cuban coastline, making low-flying passes over it. Another U.S. plane buzzes a second Cuban merchant vessel in jurisdictional waters.

October 8

Cuban President Dr. Osvaldo Dorticós Torrado asks the United Nations to condemn the actions of the United States. He denounces the aggression against Cuba and charges that the October 2 decision concerning merchant ships is an act of war which violates the UN Charter.

October 8

The head of the U.S. delegation to the UN, Adlai Stevenson, declares at a press conference after Dorticós' speech that his government reserves the right to intervene in the island, citing as a pretext the supposed "aggression in this hemisphere" and that Cuba constitutes "a collective problem for all the states of this hemisphere."

October

Tomás Gilberto Fernández Solaz, Nilo Fernández and Roberto Fuentes infiltrate in a place known as Carahatas in Las Villas. Their mission is to contact the bandit chiefs who operate in the Escambray and create an espionage network.

October

A Cuban boat is sunk in Cárdenas by cannon fire from a CIA vessel.

October 8

A S2F plane from the U.S. Air Force twice flies very low over merchant ships in waters near the Cuban coast.

October 10

An Alpha 66 commando unit attacks the town of Isabela de Sagua. A number of innocent persons are killed and others are wounded.

October 10

Counterrevolutionaries infiltrate the Santa Lucía Zone in the Province of Pinar del Río.

October 11

A large group of members of a counterrevolutionary band in Camagüey who were planning to sabotage various industries in that province are arrested. The group is headed by Samuel González Planas.

October 12
A boat attacks the north coast of Matanzas Province.

October 12
Infiltrating counterrevolutionary elements disembark near Varadero, in the northern part of Matanzas Province.

October 12
At 11:02 a.m., a U.S. plane flies just north of Santa María del Mar, on the northern coast of Havana Province.

October 13
A boat attacks, with 30 caliber machine gun fire, a pleasure craft carrying four Cubans close to Cayo Blanco near the city of Cárdenas. Filiberto Suárez Lima and Miguel Cao Medina are wounded, kidnapped by the aggressors, and taken to Miami.

October 14
A U.S. spy plane carries out a reconnaissance flight over Cuban territory and discovers ballistic missile positions in the San Cristobal region of Pinar del Río.

October 15
A vessel attacks Nueva Gerona on the Isle of Pines.

October 16-22
President Kennedy deliberates with his aides about the nuclear weapons sites in Cuba.

October 17
A U.S. fighter plane violates Cuban air space near Boca de Camarioca, on the north coast of Matanzas, and other places in the region, before leaving the island three kilometers east of Varadero.

October 21
A U-2 spy plane flies over Cuban territory.

October 21
One person is killed and six are injured as the result of pipe bomb explosions in various parts of the capital.

October 22
U.S. President John F. Kennedy orders a naval blockade of Cuba and demands that the Soviet Union withdraw all missiles and strategic weapons located on Cuban territory.

October 22
Fidel Castro orders a state of alert to prepare to combat the imminent aggression by the United States.

October 24
The U.S. naval blockade, surrounding the entire Republic of Cuba, goes into effect.

October 27
A U-2 spy plane is downed in the northern part of Oriente Province as it flies over Cuba.

October 28
Khrushchev unilaterally accepts the proposal of the U.S. President to withdraw all missiles and strategic weapons on the condition that the U.S. guarantees that there will be no aggression against Cuba.

October 29
Prime Minister of the Revolutionary Government, Commander in Chief Fidel Castro, in the name of the government and the people of Cuba, issues a communiqué containing five points or conditions required as a guarantee that there will be no aggression against Cuba on the part of the United States government:

1. End the economic blockade
2. Cease all subversive activities
3. Cease the armed attacks
4. Cease all violations of air space and territorial waters
5. Withdraw from the Guantánamo Naval Base

October 30
U Thant, Secretary-General of the United Nations, arrives in Havana and informs the press that he has come to negotiate, not to inspect. He recognized that "the sovereignty of Cuba is a basic prerequisite."

October 30
A vessel carries out an attack south of Caleta del Humo in Pinar del Río. Counterrevolutionary elements trying to infiltrate are captured.

October 30
Another vessel attacks a place known as Cayo Mambí, in the north of Oriente Province.

November 2
President Kennedy announces that the missiles stationed in Cuba are being dismantled.

November 5
The head of the Special Missions Group of the CIA, former Batista officier Miguel Angel Orozco Crespo, is captured along with another agent as they attempt a major act of sabotage in the copper mines in Pinar del Río as part of the broad plan of subversive activities outlined in Operation Mongoose.

November 14
Counterrevolutionary elements who had infiltrated south of Santiago de Cuba in Oriente are captured.

November 19
A vessel attacks the area of Jagua, south of the city of Cienfuegos.

November 20
President John F. Kennedy announces the suspension of the naval blockade against Cuba, but asserts that he will continue other aggressive political and economic measures.

November 20
U.S. planes try to sink the Cuban merchant ship *Damují*.

November 27
Another group of counterrevolutionaries who had infiltrated south of the city of Santiago de Cuba are captured.

December 1
An infiltration occurs to the east of the town of Rosario on the southern coast of Havana Province.

December 6
A vessel proceeding from the United States attacks a fishing village on the north coast of Las Villas.

December 8
Another attack, this time against the port of Caibarién.

December 21
An agent from U.S. military intelligence gives a Canadian several thousand dollars to introduce an illness that will infect Cuban turtles.

December 24
The 1,189 Cuban mercenaries captured during the Bay of Pigs invasion are freed and sent to Miami in exchange for compensation for damages suffered by the people of Cuba, in the form of $54 million in medicine and food for children.

Glossary

Artime, Manuel — Cuban counterrevolutionary and leader of the Movement for the Recovery of the Revolution (MRR). He was a CIA agent and considered one of their "golden boys."

Auténticos — Members of the Cuban Revolutionary Party (*Auténtico*) founded by Ramón Grau San Martín in 1934. They claimed to be the heirs of the Partido Revolucionario Cubano (Cuban Revolutionary Party) founded by José Martí, but their platform was both populist and demagogic. The *Auténtico* administrations of Grau (1944-1948) and Prío (1948-1952) were characterized by a high level of corruption, the proliferation of gangsterism, and submission to U.S. interests.

Batista Zaldívar, Fulgencio (1901-1973) — In 1933 he headed a military movement against the dictatorship of Gerardo Machado. He served as President of the Republic of Cuba from 1940 to 1944. In 1952 he again came to power, this time through a military coup, and he established a bloody dictatorship which was overthrown on January 1, 1959 by a popular movement led by Fidel Castro.

Casquitos — Soldiers serving the Batista tyranny, recruited during the stage of the armed insurrection to combat the rebels in the Sierra Maestra mountains. They were called *casquitos* (helmets) for the battle headgear they customarily wore.

Castro Ruz, Raúl — The brother of Fidel Castro, he was one of the young combatants who attacked the Moncada Garrison on July 26, 1953. He was imprisoned and then exiled to Mexico, where he was among the group who boarded the yacht *Granma* to return to Cuba and begin the guerrilla struggle against Batista. He formed the the Second Eastern Front. After the triumph of the revolution, he was named Minister of the Revolutionary Armed Forces and played an important role in the creation and development of the Revolutionary Armed Forces (FAR). He is Second Secretary of the Central Committee of the Communist Party of Cuba and First Vice-President of the Council of State and the Council of Ministers.

Cienfuegos, Camilo — A member of the *Granma* expedition and a combatant in the Sierra Maestra, he headed one of the two guerrilla columns bringing the revolutionary struggle from east to west. Returning to Havana in October 1959 after aborting Huber Matos' traitorous insurrection attempt, his plane was lost somewhere over the sea.

Cuban State Security — On August 22, 1958, in the Sierra Maestra mountains, Commander Raúl Castro signed a decree establishing the Servicio de Inteligencia Básica (SIR) [Basic Intelligence Service.] On January 14, 1959, at the suggestion of Commander Fidel Castro, the Departamento de Investigaciones del Ejército Rebelde (DIER) [Investigation Department of the Rebel Army] was created. On March 26, 1959, the Departamento de Información de Inteligencia de las Fuerzas Armadas Revolucionarias (DIIFAR) [Intelligence Information Department of the Revolutionary Armed Forces] was formed. On June 6, 1961, the DIER and the DIIFAR joined together under the name of the Department of State Security (DSE).

Dulles, Allen — Lawyer and director of the CIA for eight years (1953-1961) during the era of the Agency's greatest influence on U.S. foreign policy. He was the one who proposed the creation of a Special Group within the National Security Council to deal with Cuba. A few months after the Playa Girón (Bay of Pigs) fiasco, on November 28, 1961, he was dismissed from his CIA post with the following remark by President John F. Kennedy: "Your successes are unheralded . . . and your failures are trumpeted." He was also a member of the Warren Commission to investigate the 1963 assassination President John F. Kennedy.

Guevara, Ernesto "Che" — Born in Rosario, Argentina in 1928, he died in Bolivia in 1967 at the head of a guerrilla movement. He became a Cuban citizen upon the triumph of the revolution following his participation in the guerrilla struggle after joining the group of Cuban revolutionaries aboard the *Granma*. He led the Fourth Column in the march from east to west, and after the 1959 revolution held important posts in the government, contributing to its consolidation. An exemplary internationalist, he is known as "The Heroic Guerrilla."

Maceo, Antonio — Hero of the Independence Wars of the 19th century, he led a column of troops from the eastern part of the country to the west, fighting against the soldiers of the Spanish occupation. He led the Protest of Baraguá, opposing a pact which would have impeded the triumph of the insurrection, and he died in battle alongside his right-hand man, Panchito Gómez Toro.

Mella, Julio Antonio (1903-1929) — An outstanding student leader, he headed the revolutionary struggle against the dictatorship of Gerardo Machado. Creator of the Universidad Popular José Martí (José Martí Peoples' University) and the Liga Antiimperialista de Cuba (Antiimperialist League of Cuba), he was also cofounder, along with Carlos Baliño, of the Cuban Communist Party. He was assassinated in Mexico on Machado's orders.

Pérez San Román, José — An officer in Batista's army, he later became the military chief of Brigade 2506, the mercenaries who invaded at the Bay of Pigs in April 1961.

Prío Socarrás, Carlos — Elected president in 1948, his government was characterized by political and administrative corruption. He was deposed by Batista's coup d'etat on March 10, 1952.

Sánchez Arango, Aureliano — Minister of Education and of State in the Prío administration. Director of the Triple A counterrevolutionary organization in exile.

Sierra Maestra — The mountain range in Oriente Province where the guerrilla struggle against the Batista dictatorship developed.

Trujillo, Rafael Leónidas — Dominican dictator, who has also been called "the Satrap of America." He earned the nickname "Chapitas" [bottle caps] because of his taste for medals and gold braid. He organized the so-called Trujillo Conspiracy, supporting the first counterrevolutionary organization, the ill-named "White Rose," made up primarily of former soldiers of the Batista dictatorship and political hacks.

Urrutia Lleó, Manuel — A lawyer and the president of the Tribunal which judged Fidel Castro and the other Moncada assailants in 1953, in which he took an honest and honorable position in favor of the accused. In 1959 he ascended to the presidency of the country, but his wavering positions led him to have differences with the revolutionary program. He was replaced the same year by popular acclaim.

Varona Loredo, Manuel Antonio de (Tony Varona) — Prime Minister during the Prío government, he was president of the Congress and head of the Cuban Revolutionary Party (*Auténtico*) during the presidential campaign of 1948.

Vera Serafín, Aldo — Head of action and sabotage for the July 26 Movement in Havana. After the triumph of the revolution he held various important posts within the national police. A rabid anticommunist, he began very early to oppose the radical revolutionary program.

Index

Also published by Ocean Press

ISLAND UNDER SIEGE
The U.S. blockade of Cuba
by Pedro Prada
Cuban journalist Pedro Prada presents a compelling case against this "last wall" of the Cold War, showing how the 35-year blockade has affected life in the tiny island nation.

THE CUBAN REVOLUTION AND THE UNITED STATES
A chronological history
by Jane Franklin
An invaluable resource for scholars, teachers, journalists, legislators, and anyone interested in international relations, this volume offers an unprecedented vision of U.S.-Cuba relations. *Expanded second edition.*

GUANTANAMO: THE BAY OF DISCORD
The story of the U.S. military base in Cuba
by Roger Ricardo
This book provides a detailed history of the U.S. base from the beginning of the century until the present day.

FACE TO FACE WITH FIDEL CASTRO
A conversation with Tomás Borge
A lively dialogue between two of Latin America's most controversial political figures.

ZR RIFLE
The plot to kill Kennedy and Castro
by Claudia Furiati
Thirty years after the death of President Kennedy, Cuba has opened its secret files on the assassination, showing how and why the CIA, along with anti-Castro exiles and the Mafia, planned the conspiracy.

IN THE EYE OF THE STORM
Castro, Khrushchev, Kennedy and the Missile Crisis
by Carlos Lechuga
For the first time, Cuba's view of the most serious crisis of the Cold War as told by the island's ambassador to the UN.

For a list of Ocean Press distributors, see the copyright page